"My dear friend

Bobby Ka

(I am) A Real American

Memoirs of a 3rd Generation Japanese-American USAF Fighter Pilot

by

Bob Kan, Colonel USAF (Retired)

authorHOUSE®

AuthorHouse™
1663 Liberty Drive, Suite 200
Bloomington, IN 47403
www.authorhouse.com
Phone: 1-800-839-8640

First published by AuthorHouse   6/27/2008

ISBN: 978-1-4343-7373-1 (sc)

Library of Congress Control Number: 2008902206

Printed in the United States of America
Bloomington, Indiana

This book is printed on acid-free paper.

TABLE OF CONTENTS

CHAPTER 1

INTRODUCTION

This random collection of my life's anecdotes was originally intended only for my family's reference. Occasionally when I told a story to members of my family, they would say. "We never heard that before, Daddy," and would say "put your experiences in writing, Daddy, so our children can also enjoy them." Now some folks who have reviewed my draft chapters have found my stories interesting (humorous) enough to encourage me to expand the distribution.

My encounters all over the world have been interlaced with varied perceptions and assumptions regarding my Japanese-American looks and heritage. Thus, there is a lot of reference to the inference, "not really an American"....

Anecdotes include Japanese grandparents' immigration, our parents' upbringing in this new world, an incredible first flight as a seven year old; how the Pearl Harbor attack changed the lives of us Japanese-Americans; the hard times I experienced as a 9 year old selling newspapers to war-bound soldiers and sailors on the streets of Honolulu; my "home-alone" days during the war years; my routine post-war school days, my not so routine pilot training and tours as a jet training instructor; combat flight training and the tour in Vietnam; serving in Japan & Korea; working in the Middle East for a Korean company with Arabs (and Palestinians);

five years as Managing Director, McDonnell Douglas, Korea; and then consultant for Litton/TASC and Northrop Grumman Information Technology. Of great interest to my family were my personal encounters with John Wayne, Tennessee Ernie Ford, Bob Hope, and Astronaut Pete Conrad.

I am blessed with a very good memory and a watchful Guardian Angel. The stories about my adventures are factual. There is no need to make up any stories.

CAREER HISTORY

1950 – Graduated – Roosevelt High School, HNL HI

1950-1952 – Attended University of Hawaii

1954 – Married to high school sweetheart, Nancy Eto.

1952-55 – Graduate-- B.S. Education-- New York University

1955 – ROTC Commission--2/Lt USAF in Feb. Entered pilot training-- T-6 Texan

1955 – Primary Pilot Training, Graham AB FL-- Daughter Heidi, born in Marianna

1956 – T-33 Jet Training – Webb AFB TX – Daughter Vicki born in Big Spring TX.

1956-59 – Instructor Pilot (Jet) Training, Webb AFB Big Spring, TX,

1959-61 – Instructor Pilot-Williams AFB, AZ Son David born on base.

1962 – Finally, fighter training (F-84F) Moved to MacDill AFB FL (Tampa)

1963 – Nicknamed WGOFP** – World's Greatest Oriental Fighter Pilot

1963-65 – F-4 Phantom -- First USAF pilots in Phantom - Moved to Eglin AFB

1965-66 – 168 Mission Combat Tour, Ubon AB Thailand.-- Moved family to HNL

1966-69 – To Hickam (PACAF HQ) F4 Requirements Officer

1969-72 – HQ 5AF, FuchuAB Tokyo--Son Robbie born at Tachikawa AB '70.

1972-73 – Korea --80th Fighter Sq Commander (F4D) -- Family remained in Japan

1974 – Promoted to Colonel

1974-75 – Tactical Air Warfare Center -- Electronic Warfare Testing - Eglin AFB FL

1975-77 – Military Assistance Group(JUSMAG-K); 8th US Army Compound, Seoul.

1977-78 – Tactical Air Warfare Center – DCS Electronic Warfare – Eglin AFB FL

1978 – Retired from the Air Force – Joined Young Jin Enterprises in Bahrain

1978-83 – Family settled in Niceville. Bob to Bahrain; Seoul; everywhere -

1983-86 – Home to retire; Consultant with TASC; Masters at U of W FL

1986-91 – Managing Dir McDonnell Douglas, to Korea with Nan and young son Rob.

1992-2005 – Consultant, Litton-TASC, Northrop-Grumman

2006 – Commenced Extended Coffee Break in Niceville, FL Golfing, Fishing and Flying.

**WGOFP

World's Greatest Oriental Fighter Pilot (WGOFP), was a nickname given to me by my US Air Force fighter pilot comrades. Given that fighter pilots are cocky, egocentric warriors, they all regard themselves as THE WGFP (World's Greatest Fighter Pilot). There are hundreds of them, and during a typical Friday Happy Hour at the Officers' Club, one of them inserted an "O" to identify me.

The WGOFP began to fly in the T-6 Texan, Marianna, FL, Jun-Dec 55, under the great tutorship of Mr. Frank Kelley, (center) whom I consider the world's greatest flight instructor.

Next: Chapter Two – Family and Background

CHAPTER 2

FAMILY BACKGROUND

MY PARENTS

When I was descending in a parachute in Laos after the F4C fighter Joe Moran and I were flying was hit by a Soviet SA-2 missile over Hanoi, I actually thought to myself.......

"What the hell am I doing here?"

How did I get myself into this situation?

It started in Old Hawaii.

Before Pearl Harbor was attacked by Japan, we lived on the assumption that we were accepted as an American family of Japanese ancestry living in Hawaii. Pearl Harbor brought about a need for us to prove that we were patriotic Americans. In World War II the AJA's (Americans of Japanese Ancestry) proved it in their bloody battles against Germany and Italy throughout WW II. So many were superheroes, too many killed in action to prove a point, many whose parents and family were behind barbed wire fences in internment camps in the Utah Desert. Yes, many American citizens imprisoned for the duration of the war.

My parents were born in Hawaii in 1901; a year after Hawaii was annexed by the United States government to become the Territory of Hawaii, U.S.A., and therefore, THEY BOTH WERE BORN AMERICAN CITIZENS. I am their fourth child born in 1932. Hawaii remained a "Territory" of the United States, and did not become a State until 1959. Up to that time, US citizens in Hawaii were paying Federal Income Taxes without any representation in Congress. Even in 1959, there were Congressmen from the Deep South who opposed Statehood for Hawaii because Japanese were still the majority race there.

My father was the son of Japanese immigrant sugar plantation laborers and was orphaned at nine. I never learned what happened to his parents. I couldn't imagine what he, as a 9-year-old kid, went through. An "uncle" on the plantation took care of Dad for a while. He fortunately, was "adopted" by a missionary named E. E. Black and worked as a houseboy for the Black family to earn his keep. The fact that missionaries from New England "acquired" much land and wealth in Hawaii is well documented. My Dad was so lucky because the missionaries provided him the best education available, and in 1919 he emerged as the second Oriental to earn a college degree in Hawaii. He became a well-respected certified (Normal School) schoolteacher and a staunch Christian at 20 years of age. My Bible-toting Dad (who sang "Jesus Loves me This I know," in the shower) taught on the island of Maui where he met my mother. In addition, the E.E. Blacks allowed my Dad to attend Japanese language school on the plantation following regular school, and my father learned to speak, read and write Japanese at the high school level. My father was the model "Golden Man" in Hawaii as described by James Michner in his super-novel HAWAII; someone who was comfortable in both Far-Eastern and Western societies. He was quite adept in old fashioned Japanese calligraphy.

William S. Kan, 1924

<u>Side story – Shirley Temple</u>. Years later, following her divorce to actor John Agar, a very young teen-ager named Shirley Temple took refuge at the same EE Black plantation home on the Big Island of Hawaii, and in her recluse, met and eventually married a son, Charlie Black. The reason I mention this is I often refer, tongue in cheek, to the fact that I am related to Shirley Temple Black, albeit remotely and unofficially.

<u>My Mom</u> was born in Wailuku in 1901, on the island of Maui. Her father, Yosaburo Kido was above being an ordinary sugar-cane field laborer. "Oji-san" left the cane fields and became a self-employed stonecutter and his major projects were engraving Japanese characters on solid rock tombstones and caretaker of a nearby Japanese cemetery. Following the end of the WW II, he mysteriously took off for Japan and quickly came back as some kind of priest, a Shaman, a spin-off of the Shinto religion.

Whereupon "Oji-san" set up a small shrine adjoining his house and began consultation and prayer services for "clients." He dramatically performed the high priest hocus-pocus waving of white paper streamers, sounding of bells and gongs and reciting sutras. His Japanese clients consulted with him about their particular problem(s). Through my grandfather, his "clients" got "messages" from deceased ancestors sometimes at graveside. After his praying, he would sit with the people and advise them about the proper course(s) of action based on his "conversations" with the dead. Most often, the same people would return and make monetary offerings and would deliver rice, barrels of soy sauce (shoyu) and other merchandise in gratitude for Grandpa's "wizardry." He earned enough to purchase a two story house with a separate bath house.

When there was no longer a requirement for his "counsel" in Maui (perhaps his clients got wise), granpa "Oji-San" Kido sold the Wailuku property and moved to Honolulu.

My brother found a job for him as a janitor In a government office, in which he earned enough credits to qualify for Social Security benefits.…… a significant quirk in U.S. government generosity to aliens.

Grandma Take Kido became ill and then blind, then passed away. Sometime later around 1960, Granpa Yosaburo decided to return to his home village in Kumamoto, Japan. He lived very well there on his U.S. Social Security benefits in post-war years in Japan. He became known as the "Hawaii King" because he could afford a big house on the top of a hill overlooking his village. His was the only home with a western-style running water toilet. My dad and mom, brother and his wife visited Grandpa in '62, then in his eighties, and bedridden. He had married a retired nurse, the widow of his younger brother and, they adopted a young girl (a relative). After Yosaburo died, both his widow and adopted daughter continued to receive Social Security benefits. (until the widow died and the daughter reached the age of 18).

Photos: My grandparents Yosaburo and Take Kido and my mother in 1902. I enhanced this photo above by super-imposing them on Wailuku, Maui (A Bishop Museum photo), my mother's birthplace. Bottom photo is of my Mom in 1926.

Back to my Mom: Following the War, my brother Sid became a law stenographer. In 1975 he found some old court records on our Mom's home island of Maui that revealed that she was previously married. It was an "arranged" marriage to an older man. When my brother confronted her with this knowledge (50 years after the fact), my Mom broke into tears. She and my Dad had kept it a "deep, dark" secret from the family. I happened to be in Honolulu to celebrate my parent's 50th Wedding Anniversary at that time, and was at their house when this fact was revealed. As my Mom was sobbing, my brother asked me, "Hey Bob, did you know Mom was married once, before she met Dad?," and I replied nonchalantly, "Oh yeah?," and then carried on a conversation on another subject. My pretense of unconcern surprised my Mom, and my brother said, "see, Mom, no one cares if you were married before." It sobered her and she was so relieved.

Later, she told my sister Kats that when she saw our Dad, she was so attracted to him that she filed for divorce, left her first husband, and aggressively pursued our Dad.

Another "secret" was she had a son from this previous marriage who died in his infancy. She saved his little bones and kept them in a jar in her closet at home. In 1996, a year before she died, she asked my sister Kats to include these bones in the cremation of her remains. So her urn in the mausoleum in Honolulu now contains ashes of the two. Except for Kats, no one heard anything about this until July 22, 2005, when Kats told me about it in a telecon while I was doing my family background research. Had I not decided to write memoirs, these facts about my unique mother might have never been revealed.

Urns – My Dad and Mom + 1 – Nuuanu, Honolulu

<u>Palolo Valley Home</u>: My Dad's teaching assignments took him from island to island, from Maui to the big island of Hawaii, then finally to Honolulu where he taught at the Ala Moana School for Retarded Children (Later euphemistically called the Vocational School for the Mentally Challenged) for the rest of his teaching years. I used to hate it when he jokingly introduced me to his friends as a star pupil at his school.

When they settled in Honolulu (about 1930), my Dad bought a home on Palolo Avenue, in a relatively nice multi-racial neighborhood; a three-bedroom, one-bath house on an acre of land for $6700.

In spite of hard national economic times, because he was a certified school teacher, my Dad was able to obtain a mortgage for almost the full amount. The Palolo Stream bordered our land in the back yard, and it was very nice.

So it took 15 years to pay off the mortgage, and our family's activities were focused entirely during that period on paying for the property. I will later describe how I made $2 a day as a newsboy at 9 years of age and it all went to paying off the mortgage. I worked every summer, as a newsboy, caring for neighbor's lawns, raising chickens, etc. For three summers I worked at the Dole Pineapple cannery on the early shift and then at the Queen's Hospital in the evenings. My brother and sisters worked during their "leisure times" in various jobs.

One of the most memorable, joyful scenes involving my parents was when the last mortgage payment was made in 1945. My father had just returned home from making the final payment at Honolulu Savings and Loan and was sitting on his rocking chair in the living room.

It was coincidentally, the end of World War II, so there was much to celebrate. When my Dad announced that the house was "ours," my Mom rushed him to hug him, and toppled the rocking chair backwards. Luckily no one was hurt. Just a lot of laughs and joy. As part of the celebration, my Dad bought a brand new 1945 Chevrolet.

In later chapters, I write more about my Mom, who certainly was not the average mother.

Ten years before my Dad retired as a schoolteacher, my mother planted a dozen plumeria trees in the front and back yards. My Dad thought it was "pupule" (crazy idea). My mom didn't tell him why she was planting these trees, and it was later that it dawned on him that she was creating a retirement job for him. He was thinking of working as a night watchman. The plumeria is nicknamed the "graveyard flower," as they are found in many graveyards in Hawaii. The fragrant white, pink, red or white plumeria flowers are used to make "leis" that are traditional gifts, expressions of "aloha" for arriving and departing visitors. In those ten years the plants grew into fifteen foot sprawling, prolific trees and each produced hundreds of flowers every day. Her timing was great. The trees matured when my Dad retired.

Mom instructed him to build scaffolds around every tree to expedite flower gathering, and to preclude him from falling. She had him buy two large refrigerators, big plastic bags, and instructed him how to build a comfortable lei making workbench.

For the next twenty years, my father worked two hours a day earning close to $2000 per month in addition to his teacher's pension. The lei vendors paid $1.25 per lei, and my Dad had practically no overhead expenses. They used this income for travel to the Orient and Las Vegas. They loved the California Hotel in downtown Vegas.

Another example of my Mom's ingenuity....She noticed that there were some Japanese students across the Palolo Stream praying. They were foreign students attending the Chaminade College nearby and because they were of the Shinto faith, they had to worship away from the Catholic school.

So Mom asked my Dad to build a Shinto Shrine in our back yard. Again, my Dad called it another hair-brained "pupule" idea. This time my Mom couldn't overcome my Dad's obstinacy so the idea was dropped.

Mom's motivation for this "project" was there is a 100% State of Hawaii real estate tax exemption for anyone who had a religious shrine on his property.

Mother died eight years after my Dad at age 96. There was no funeral, according to her will. On my last visit to see her, she surprised everyone by recalling detailed events of my childhood. She said, "You were a good boy, Bobby."

It was one huge emotional moment for me that afternoon flying back to Florida, as I looked down at Palolo Valley from the departing airliner....

Next: Chapter 3 – My First Flight

CHAPTER 3

MY FIRST FLIGHT IN 1939

My mother was quite influential in formulating and perpetuating my life's ambitions. In the thirties, except for his occasional fatherly lectures and his signing of my report cards, my Dad was too involved in making ends meet and paid little attention to me.

From the time I first saw numerous Army Air Corps fighters flying over Honolulu skies, I talked incessantly about wanting to be a pilot. So one day, when I was 7 years old and unbeknownst to my Dad, my Mom arranged for me to fly in a private light aircraft at John Rodgers Airport (now known as Honolulu International). She had surreptitiously saved coins in a mayonnaise jar that she hid in a compartment in the kitchen cupboard where she also kept some homemade wine derived from our own grapevine. (I used to occasionally sneak a sip. Yummy.) She used the coins to pay a crusty old unkempt gray-moustached pilot to fly me in his Piper Cub. I don't know how much she had saved, but the old pilot assessed that it was enough for about 40 minutes of airtime. I also have no idea how my Mom came up with this deal and how she got off from pineapple cannery job that day.

On the way to the airport in the bus, she gave me a "good luck" piece to wear around my neck. It was a piece of paper with Buddhist prayers written within, wrapped in purple and white cloth tied to a string.

I climbed into the front seat; the pilot sat immediately behind me and flew from the back seat. We took off and flew off shore, just south of Barber's Point, and he showed me the Chandelle (a precision diving and climbing 180 degree turn maneuver) and Lazy Eight, flight maneuvers that I actually had to perform much later in pilot training. I was not comfortable because of some flight turbulence caused by the famous Hawaiian trade winds flowing up and over the island's Koolau Range, but overall it produced my first real "high," and immediately after landing, I reaffirmed to my Mom my desire to become a pilot.

As we departed, I remember the pilot commenting what a lucky kid I was.

When I takeoff today in light aircraft, the sounds and sensations are still so reminiscent of that flight in 1939. Since '39 and today, I accumulated over 5000 thrilling and enjoyable pilot hours in mostly supersonic jet fighter and trainer aircraft. Thanks, Mom.

I started on a 90 mph Piper Cub in '39, and now in my post-retirement in '07, I'm tooling around in a Cessna 172 at 110 mph. Isn't that real progress?

I wore that same Buddhist purple and white good luck piece around my neck on all of my 168 combat missions in Vietnam. I still have it somewhere with all of my memorabilia.

In retrospect, I still marvel at Mom's insight…. This Dole pineapple cannery laborer with a sixth grade education, entrusting her seven year old son's life to a maverick pilot (probably uninsured), when everyone else in the family was working his/her butt off to make ends meet in the late years of the Great Depression……

Who would've thought?..... I am forever in awe and so grateful to Mom. My Dad obviously was never informed about that flight, and I just recently told my siblings about it along with some of my other old secrets.

Next: Chapter 4 -- Pearl Harbor Saga – A different perspective --

CHAPTER 4

THE ATTACK ON PEARL HARBOR – A 9 YEAR OLD'S PERSPECTIVE

Have vivid memories as I watched Pearl Harbor being attacked by the Imperial Japanese Navy on December 7, 1941. Life changed drastically for most Americans; and for us Americans of Japanese ancestry, IT WAS TRAUMATIC.

I hated Japan (still do) for upsetting our lives and making much of the American public, including President Roosevelt, look at us Japanese-Americans as "enemies."

We used to know Pearl Harbor as a Fun Place: A year or two before the attack on Pearl Harbor, my family was invited by my Dad's friends to join them in a time share of a two-story house on the water on the north end of Pearl Harbor owned by a Japanese alien. If it existed today, that house would be across the highway from the Pearl Shopping Center in the vicinity of the watercress farms, with an electric power plant in the vicinity. I remember the pools of cool, clear artesian water just a few yards in-land. There were large colorful Japanese carp swimming in those pools. We and two other families used the time-share on the first Sunday of each month. The brackish water on the north shore of Pearl Harbor was unpolluted in 1939-41 and we swam there and ate the seafood we harvested. The kids fished from the dock with bamboo poles catching numerous little edible perch-like fish. Quickly scaled with heads and belly removed and fried tempura style, they were a delicious, crunchy mouthful. There was an abundance of clams in the muddy flats on the Ewa (west) side and my brother caught small hammerhead sharks and I think they were sold to Chinese restaurants for their fins. They made a delicacy called Shark-fin Soup.

On <u>November 31, 1941</u>, my Dad's friends were informed by the Japanese proprietor that the time-share house would not be available on the following Sunday.

No reason was given, and we never saw the proprietor again.

I intriguingly speculate (have no proof) that this proprietor was *Takeo Yoshikawa,*

<u>THE #1 JAPANESE SPY</u>, who reported all USN ship activity to Japan. From the second floor balcony of that house, one had a clear view of battleship row and binoculars were not even required. In the movie, *Pearl Harbor,* the "SPY" was a dentist whose office was on the slopes of Pearl City overlooking Pearl Harbor.

Just recently I read in a historical article that Yoshikawa was apprehended by the FBI in Honolulu and transported to the mainland for interrogation and confinement. He returned to Japan after the war and died unheralded.

So on the morning of December 7th we remained at our Palolo Avenue home. I was catching "medaka" (minnows) in the stream in our back yard when I heard the explosions. Boom-boom-boom and Boom! I followed some curious folks downstream, then up to the hill to the St. Louis school campus and from there we saw the smoke filled air over Pearl Harbor and Hickam Air Base, some ten miles away. I saw what I learned later were Japanese fighter-bombers doing their thing. We didn't see the US Army Air Force P-40s defending as was shown in the movie *Pearl Harbor.*

I wasn't supposed to have wandered that far away from home, so I quickly returned home. My family was listening to the radio. Webley Edwards, on KGMB, one of two radio stations, warned, "This is not an exercise, do not leave your home, we are being attacked by the Japanese….."

There were some fanatic Japanese aliens who "banzai-ed" and raised the Japanese flags at their homes, including our alien neighbor, Mr. Tanaka. These folks were quickly apprehended by the feds. They didn't take Mrs. Tanaka.

A few days following the attack my father was allowed to drive down to the Ala Moana School where he taught, to check on the facilities. It was located on the water adjacent to the US Army's Ft. Armstrong near Honolulu Harbor. Upon arrival, my Dad heard a shot, and saw that an old Hawaiian man was lying on the beach. My Dad went to help, only to find the man dead, shot by a trigger-happy sentry at the Fort. My Dad said the old man was on his usual stroll along the beach.

The police confiscated short-wave radios, and everyone was ordered to black out their windows so no light could be seen at night. Auto headlights were blacked out with a hood and only a sliver of light could be projected.

President Roosevelt had a notion to order total evacuation of ALL Japanese-Americans in Hawaii and interning them in desert camps in Arizona, Nevada and Utah. However, the Military Governor in Hawaii told Roosevelt that there were too many, so the idea was abandoned.

It was a dismal two months before we returned to school.

OUR RETURN TO SCHOOL AFTER PEARL HARBOR

When we returned to school, most of our non-Japanese friends were nice. There were a few who called the Japanese-Americans kids "spies," "dirty Japs," and such, but what they said was only a reflection of what they heard at their homes.

Hawaii was under martial law, and all civilians were issued gas masks. We were briefed that the Japanese may use mustard gas or other "WEAPONS OF MASS DESTRUCTION." Actually, mustard gas affects the skin so the mask didn't matter. Unless one had a fat face, the masks didn't fit us kids anyway. It was just a token US Army effort. We were forced to carry those oversized gas masks in hideous GI bags. After a few months, most kids left their gas masks at home and carried food or books in the bag. Periodically, we had to test our masks in a tear gas chamber. As tightly as we pulled the straps, and even with additional sponge lining, the masks leaked. We always came out with eyes smarting like hell. My Mom was so worried about the futility of the issued gas mask, she fashioned a heavy gauze mask on the sewing machine for me. It probably would have worked better than the GI issue.

PHOTO: Kids in the fourth grade with gas masks. I'm the little kid in the middle In the dark shirt.

Another very unpleasant experience for all of us school kids was the mandatory air raid drills. Early on, the trenches were cut in the schoolyard, and after a rain, the trenches were a pool of mud. Later, bomb shelters were built, but rainwater also accumulated in the shelters. During the air raid drills, we were all forced to get into the muddy trenches and later bomb shelters, and it was unbelievably mucky. Our nice school shoes and socks were soaked in mud.

The teachers got wise and allowed the kids to take their shoes and socks off before entering the shelter during those practice drills. Our clothes were always soiled during these stupid drills because we had to sit on dirty benches in the shelters. At Kapalama Elementary where my wife went to school, teacher Mrs. Honea's dress shrunk in the rain as the student's observed in disbelief during one of those drills in the rain.

We were nine year olds who hated Japan for attacking Pearl Harbor, but lucky that Japan did not follow-up with an invasion.

Every one of our classmates on Oahu at the time Pearl Harbor was attacked has his/her own unique dramatic experiences vividly imbedded in their minds. We all do *Remember Pearl Harbor* and there are many stories that should be chronicled.

In '41 there were many classmates from the mainland whose parents were either US military or civilian businessmen.

Us "locals" were so preoccupied by our own apprehensions that we never thought about what they went through.

We had classmates like Ted Vento and Wini Guyer Harbeson who had harrowing experiences and are, in fact, truly combat veterans. There are many other stories to tell.

Before the recent Dec 7th anniversary, I asked Wini and Ted about their Pearl Harbor experiences. We were classmates since early elementary school days, but until now I never knew of their perilous times as 9 year olds.

With their permission, I condensed their stories to facilitate publication.

OUR US NAVY KIDS' PEARL HARBOR EXPERIENCES:

<u>Wini Guyer Harbeson's story</u>: "After a few months, the government asked all folks (especially women and children) from the mainland to leave the islands if they could…. (we) were taken by a converted luxury ship to San Diego…..The ship (Lurline) was the fastest in the Pacific Ocean and could outrun a Japanese submarine. Our boys that had been wounded were all lined up on the decks, row after row of them.. we had brought lots of comics to read and gave them to the wounded service men…most were very young and were so grateful for something to read. Mom took two other girls with us and we were crammed into a stateroom built for two. We had three bunks on either side, 6 stuffed in that little staterooms. I was very sick with seasickness. We had only saltwater to bathe with and ate a lot of dehydrated eggs and potatoes. We had drills everyday and everyone had to go up on deck and put on his or her life preservers. I would lay in the gutter and throw up, too sick to care. Finally, we arrived in San Diego. Our ship had to wait for the nets to open. <u>As we were waiting, a Japanese sub torpedoed us! (It imbedded in the hull.) Fortunately it was a dud...</u>"

<u>Ted Vento</u>: "On 12/7/41 I was staying the weekend with friends of my folks at Damon Tract….along side the fence of John Rodgers

Airport...we had a good view of planes over Hickam...and much black flak smoke all over.....we were shooed inside by a HNL PD cop....and right away a Japanese plane made a strafing run over the neighborhood.... hitting the house we were in... a couple of bullets....must have been small caliber....did not make very big holes.

We were ordered to go back to the mainland but had to wait for a ship....yes the Lurline, the same ship we had come over on in about 1936.....We finally left on the Lurline...now painted an awful grey in May of 42. We had a destroyer escort back to San Francisco...I am sure it was needed as that was the time that the Battle of Midway took place....and now hearing of Wini's torpedoing...they had good reason to send an escort......In 1946 we returned to Pearl Harbor...my Dad had gotten shore duty there I attended 9th grade at Pearl Harbor school.

I then rejoined classmates at Roosevelt in the 10th grade...fall of 1947....and now you know the rest of the story."

Next: Chapter 5: My First Job

CHAPTER 5

MY FIRST JOB.
AGE 9. SUMMER OF '42

I don't really know what my Mom's motivation was when she got me a newsboy's job in downtown Honolulu in 1942. It wasn't like sending a son to summer camp. Perhaps it was her way of transforming a naive boy into a man, but perhaps it was pure economics. My father was a school teacher and he decided to buy a house on one acre of land plus raising 4 children on his salary. As I mentioned earlier this necessitated everyone in the family to pitch in. My Mom had to go to work at the local pineapple-canning factory. Jobs for local women with limited education were very few, and working at the canneries was one of the options. My Mom incredibly got me that newsboy's job. I subcontracted to a father-less teen-ager, whose family was (also) struggling for survival. He docked a penny per paper sold for the privilege of working in his territory, which was in the busiest part of Honolulu. The papers cost five cents each, and ordinarily a newsboy made 2 cents per paper. So I netted a penny per paper making $2 a day at the most. I peddled newspapers on the south (Makai) side of Hotel & Richard Streets where thousands of unruly soldiers and sailors wandered about looking for "entertainment" before they were off to war in the Pacific, with the realization of not surviving and returning from the war zone. I heard later that Ben Wood sold morning papers on the Mauka side. I don't recall seeing him.

Hotel Street was the vice-center of Honolulu and it was lined with honky-tonk beer joints and houses of ill repute. Prostitution was illegal there then as it is now, but what was a city to do, full of feelings of patriotism and gratitude to thousands of these fighting men stopping in HNL before going off to dangerous/life-threatening war zones in the Pacific? The city authorities either looked the other way, or perhaps were involved in that "business."

I sold about 100 to 200 papers per day to mostly servicemen, and I handed the full amount earned to my Dad when I got home every day, minus the twenty-five cents I occasionally was allowed to spend for a hamburger and a soda for lunch.

I carried twenty-five newspapers at a time and walked the side-walks calling out, "Paaa-per---Star-Bullllll-e-tinn!" GI's shouted at me: "Hey kid, you got a sister I can f__k?" Being just 9 years old, I had no idea what that meant. When I asked at the dinner table, Mom's answer was, "It means kissing, Bobby." It wasn't until later that my fourth grade classmate Freddie Murata told me the real meaning of the word. While Freddie was educating me, one of the girls in our class heard Fred say the "f" word, and tattled to the teacher, Mrs. Adelaide Stearns. She got hold of Fred and literally washed his mouth out with soap. Teachers could do that in those days.

I found out much later from older boys why sailors and soldiers were standing in a long line on Hotel St near Mauna Kea St. The line led up a flight of stairs. Up the stairs were two or three prostitutes "servicing" these service men, each one performing the world's record shortest "short-timer" for a few dollars. I was told by the older boys (how did they know?) that it was done rapidly, the woman standing up doggy style, accommodating one after another. These women incredibly did hundreds of men a day. The servicemen often remarked as they came out, "I didn't even know what she looked like," and all she said was "next!"

GROSS! War is Hell.

Quite frequently, I heard, "Beat it you Jap kid," or "Watch him, he might have a knife behind those newspapers."

One day, in front of the Black Cat Cafe, when I held a paper in front of a sailor, he slapped the newspapers out of my hands, soiling all of them. I yelled at him as he smiled and walked away, and then I cried, as I would have to pay for them. Standing on the corner at the Richard Street bus stop was the city bus company's supervisor in a black uniform carrying the bus schedules on a clip board, checking on the movement of busses as they passed through. He was a big bus supervisor by day, and he was Vilai Su'a, the giant Samoan professional wrestler by night.

He noticed me crying as I walked by, and asked:

"Hey, wassamatter, kid?" I told him what the sailor had done. "Show me the guy," he said, so I took Vilai up some stairs into the Black Cat Cafe where I identified the sailor standing at the bar having a bottle of Primo beer. Vilai ordered the sailor to pay me for all of the papers, and when the sailor scoffed and said something like "go to hell," Vilai grabbed him and threw him violently into the bar. Several other sailors who had rushed him also got thrown against the bar. He was so strong; he manhandled the sailors as if they were children. I had never seen such violence before.

He then with one hand picked up that dazed sailor by the floppy sailor uniform collar and made him pay me two dollars, more than what the soiled papers were worth. As we walked out of the saloon, Vilai said, "Hey kid, anybody gives you any trouble, you tell me, ok?"

What luck. I HAD THE STRONGEST MAN ON THE ISLAND AS MY BODYGUARD!

After my parents heard about some of my on-the-job experiences, they decided that they would find something else for me to do the following summers. ....but what an experience it was for a 9 year old.

Awesome memories.

(See photos of my "workplace" below.)

A 1942 Bishop Museum photo of the Black Cat Cafe as I knew it. I met Vilai Su'a in front of Pacific Jewelers. The Black Cat was on the second floor.

Where the seedy Black Cat once stood is the prestigious Alii Palace. Many of Honolulu's most distinguished law firms have their offices there today.

(My photo below.)

Just over fifty years later, in almost the exact location where Vilai Su'a beat up the sailor who called me a "dirty Jap kid," my nephew had his office as one of the Hawaii State Prosecuting Attorneys. My nephew was the assistant DA for 19 years, then became an Ordained Luteran Minister. (another story)

Only in America!

October 14, 2005--The same, exact location above on Hotel St.

Army-Navy YMCA across the street from the Black Cat Cafe. Circa 1942 (Bishop Museum Photo). Richard St. just to the Right.

The same location on October 14, 2005. It is the same building refurbished. It now houses the Hawaii State Art Museum.

Next: Chapter 6 – War vs the Mongoose

CHAPTER 6

THE MONGOOSE

THE SUMMER OF '43 – WAR VS THE MONGOOSE

While I was peddling newspapers in downtown Honolulu in June of '42, the US Navy was victorious in the great Battle of Midway. It was the turning point of the war and the Japanese were turned away from Hawaii. Folks who weren't confined to barbed wire enclosed detention camps started to return to the islands. The 442nd Regimental Combat Team and 100th Infantry Battalions (Americans of Japanese Ancestry) were deployed to Europe.

In the following summer of '43, following that outlandish summer on Hotel and Richard Streets, my parents decided it was safer to keep me at home. I was "home-alone" on Palolo Avenue for the next two summers, as my parents and two sisters all had summer jobs. My brother was in the mainland, an interpreter in the US Army. Because he had skipped a grade in elementary school, he was one year younger than his McKinley High classmates (like Medal of Honor recipient Senator Daniel Inouye). He was too young to join the initial deployment of the Americans of Japanese Ancestry (AJA) who made up the famous and heroic 100th Battalion and the 442nd Regimental Combat Team. As brother Sid had just completed 12 years of Japanese schooling he was sent to a US Army school for interpreters and prisoner interrogators. My Mom was so relieved that my brother was not assigned to a combat unit. I was in the third grade and was overjoyed to hear that our Japanese schools were terminated after Pearl Harbor. I hated it when we had to bow to the "Kocho-Sensei" (Japanese Principal) and sing the Japanese national anthem. In retrospect I realize that rather than just teaching us Japanese culture, they were actually trying to influence our loyalties. They were successful with some of the Japanese-Americans.

My Dad built outdoor and indoor chicken coops in the back yard and gave me the job of incubating and raising chickens and ducks, mainly to have a meat and egg supply for the family, some income, and something for me to do over the summer vacation.

Beef and pork were rationed at Honolulu markets through most of the war. With much of the available fresh meat being consumed by the armed forces, SPAM became very popular in Hawaii as it was abundantly available to us. Tourists visiting Hawaii today wonder why SPAM and eggs, SPAM sushi and teriyaki SPAM are so popular in Hawaii. We were brought up with SPAM.

While I was "home-alone," I was forbidden to wander too far from home. Fortunately, I was able to spend some spare time with the musically talented Hawaiian boys at the nearby "Triangle Park" where I picked up an extensive repertoire of Hawaiian music, singing and learning to play the ukulele. Those big guys accepted me as part of their "gang," perhaps because they enjoyed the mangoes and papayas I used to bring them from our trees in our backyard. It was a good feeling to "belong," and to have their "protection" from neighborhood bullies.

I got to play a little sandlot baseball due to the kindness of one Albert Pagan, who let me play in the outfield. I was using an old discarded, dry baseball glove I found that didn't even have a pocket. Al managed the team, played shortstop and was the best hitter. In one crucial memorable play, there was a hit into shallow left field, Albert went back and got a glove on the ball but it bounced off his fingertips. I was there backing him to catch the ricochet for the out. I'll never forget the praise I got from my friend Al. He is presently a retired Air Force Chief Master Sergeant and a great-grandfather. Super guy.

In a contrasting activity, I also occasionally "wandered" a few doors the other way and visited with three wonderful and beautiful teen-aged sisters who taught me the "social graces," including dancing "fox trot" and "boogie-woogie" to the music of Glenn Miller, Artie Shaw, etc. Their father was a successful merchant in Honolulu, and their mother was an attractive Filipino actress often commuting to Manila. I am so grateful to the sisters for their graciousness and their "tutoring" as I was growing through the impressionable ages of 11 and 12. Pleasant memories.

MY SUMMER JOB AND OUR WAR AGAINST THE MONGOOSE

My home job assignment, my primary mission, was to care for the fifty or so chickens and ducks in the coops my Dad built in our spacious back yard. The work included maintaining the facilities and keeping them clean. The chicken manure was useful in fertilizing our veggie gardens. Dad also bought an incubator and taught me how to identify fertile eggs and I hatched chicks. It was fun to watch the chicks emerge from the eggshell. So cute.

Selling poultry and eggs would be my source of income for some time to come. When any one of our neighbors wanted a fresh chicken for dinner, I would catch a rooster, kill it by slitting its throat, drain as much blood as I could out of the dying cock's throat, soak it in hot water, feather it, dress and deliver it receiving a total of fifty cents for the effort. Our large, fresh brown Rhode Island Red chicken eggs sold for twenty-five cents a dozen.

A tough task I had was to guard the chickens, ducks and newly hatched chicks from the dreaded MONGOOSE.

Mongoose Background:

The small Indian Mongoose was imported to Hawaii in 1883 to eliminate a growing number of "illegal immigrant" rats and snakes that scampered or slithered down ship tie-down lines or came in the crates offloaded from foreign ships at Honolulu Harbor.

It appeared to be a good idea as the mongoose was successful in eliminating the snakes and stemming the wide spread growth of the rat population, particularly in the sugar cane fields where the rats were consuming and spoiling the sugar cane crops.

.....But it backfired. The "solution" became as large a problem as the original one. The mongoose, without a natural enemy in Hawaii, flourished quickly and insidiously throughout most of the islands. Unimpeded, the mongoose created havoc in the balance of nature in Hawaii. It was recently described as an ecological terrorist, on the verge of completely eliminating the State Nene Bird (a type of goose), and the Hawkbill turtle, as well as many other species of birds by sucking up the eggs and devouring the offspring. The only predator-enemy the mongoose has in Hawaii is man. The mongoose looks very much like a ferret with the sharpest teeth and claws.

So in those early forties, as an eleven year old, I was tasked to defend our chickens and ducks against the mongoose threat. The mongoose thrived along the Palolo Stream that flowed beyond our property boundary and the rodents had free access to our properties.

After we continued to lose chickens and eggs to the mongoose, my Dad built Rube Goldberg-like box-traps with little entrances that closed when the mongoose pulled on a stick wrapped with meat inside the box.

It worked well, and when one was trapped, Dad would place a burlap bag at the opening, slide open the door, and the mongoose would run into the bag. He would then quickly close and tie the bag, and then strike the bag into a stonewall vigorously and repeatedly until the mongoose was dead. We had to be careful as the mongoose had sharp teeth, it was quick and many were said to be rabid.

Our traps caught dozens and we must have wiped out the Palolo Stream mongoose population, as they eventually stopped coming.

Now comes the bizarre part. Our neighbor, the Hibinos, (a Japanese Alien couple) owned a hat and leather goods store on the plush Fort Street shopping area in Honolulu. They were allowed to remain in

Honolulu by the Feds to continue their business after Pearl Harbor as they were quiet residents and minded their own business. The Hibinos had a Persian cat.

Well, one morning a situation emerged. Their beautiful Persian cat came wandering into our yard while I was gathering eggs and feeding the chickens and ducks. Also, I had noticed that the mongoose trap door was closed, and a mongoose was trapped in it. I usually would wait for Dad to come home to kill the mongoose. However, I had another one of my absolutely "brilliant" ideas. I would let the cat perform the execution, I thought. There was an empty chicken coop available, a perfect "battle arena," for the drama. I knew that cats could kill rats… and assumed that the Persian cat could handle the mongoose, which looked like a large rat. The coop was about 15 X 15 feet, enclosed by a six-foot high chicken wire fence. So I carried the mongoose trap into the coop, and then enticed the cat into the enclosure and opened the trap door. Almost instantly, the mongoose had the cat by its throat and tore it open with its sharp teeth. The cat died instantly. I was shocked! In a panic, I managed to corner the mongoose before he climbed over the six foot fence and with one lucky blow with a shovel, killed it instantly. So there lay two little animals, the cat with its throat ripped open, and the dead mongoose, its head soaked with cat's blood. After I gathered my wits, I covered up the "murder scene." I dug a deep hole in a remote corner of the back yard on the slope away from the chicken coop and buried the two animals together and concealed the "grave" neatly with rocks, soil and leaves. I then washed all the blood away from the coop with a garden hose, and everything looked normal again. I then rebaited the trap with chicken gizzards and replaced it in its normal place with the door open. Later that day, I heard Mrs. Hibino call "Neko-san" ("neko" means kitty or cat in Japanese) and when she saw me, she inquired in Japanese, "Bobby-san, have you seen my Neko?"

(I am) A Real American

Of course, my answer was, "No, Ma'm." I never told anyone about my fight promotion, the awesome quickness of the mongoose and how in just a matter of seconds it slaughtered Mrs. Hibino's pedigreed cat. Not until the year 2000, 57 years later did I tell my siblings. My sister Kats, exclaimed, "I was wondering all these years what happened to Mrs. Hibino's cat." Sister Aileen couldn't believe it, and my brother, who was away in '43, was amused. My Dad & Mom never knew.

Next: Chapter 7 – A short look at School Days

41

CHAPTER 7

SCHOOL DAYS –ROUTINE

My post-war school days through high school and two years at the University of Hawaii were happy and enjoyable, but mostly uneventfully routine.

I was a so-so varsity basketball and baseball player for three years, editor of the The Rough Rider, the bi-weekly Roosevelt High School paper, and had a tiny solo stint in the 300 voice A Cappella Choir that none of my classmates could recall. I played basketball on the University of Hawaii Freshman and Junior Varsity teams. My grades were an average 2.5 at the U of Hawaii but upon transfer to New York University it escalated to 4.0 (straight A's). I must have matured.

I graduated from New York University with a B.S. in Education and commissioned a 2nd Lieutenant on Feb 14, 1955, and entered the USAF on May 7th.

The most memorable school event was meeting the beautiful Nancy Eto in high school, who eventually became my wife in 1954.

Next: Chapter 8 – Air Force Stories

CHAPTER 8

AIR FORCE STORIES

PRIMARY FLYING TRAINING
IN THE DEEP SOUTH

Following my commissioning as a 2nd Lieutenant at the New York University Air Force ROTC, I followed my childhood ambition to become a fighter pilot, and my pregnant wife, Nan, and I found us in Marianna FL, at Graham Air Base Primary Pilot Training School. Marianna is a small town north of Panama City in Northwest FL. The entire NW Florida area was popularly known, even today, as "LA" or "Lower Alabama."

My oldest daughter, Heidi was born there in 1955. In 1955, the "Colored" (Blacks) were still very much second class citizens, and were suffering the indignities of riding in the back of busses, using separate restroom facilities and other forms of segregation. That is the main reason my Black ROTC classmates at New York University did not sign up for pilot training because ALL of the available USAF pilot training bases were in the Deep South.

One afternoon, wife Nan and I drove to downtown Marianna to shop at the Ben Franklin Five & Dime store. While browsing through the store, I noticed that there were two separate drinking fountains with prominent signs, WHITE and COLORED on them. The white store manager happened to be standing there cordially welcoming us. I was in uniform, and he could see that I was a USAF 2nd Lieutenant.

I pointed to the drinking fountains and asked: "Which one do I drink from, Sir?"

The manager scratched his head and replied, "Well you ain't Colored, so you must be White! Go ahead and drink from the White one." There were two"Colored" employees in the store, and they heard the manager, obviously keeping their thoughts to themselves.

I smiled and thanked the manager, but I didn't drink any water there.

Note: I must say that we have never been treated discourteously or with disrespect here in the Deep South. Before the mid-sixties, inter-racial marriage was prohibited in most of the South, even between Asians and Whites. All four of our children eventually married Caucasians. In '77 my second daughter, Vicki, married Barry Kendrick, a high school local boy in Niceville FL, whose kin are from central Alabama and whose ancestors were in the Confederate Army. The kids could not have inter-married back in earlier days. Vicki has been adored by that family, especially by Barry's grandparents and generally by the wonderful people from Central Alabama.

Once in a while, being the only non-Caucasian among 250 pilot trainees, I would encounter a curious local person. One old farmer in Two-Egg, Alabama, in coveralls, straw hat and smoking a corncob pipe (no kidding), asked me, "Where're you from, Son?" I replied "Honolulu, Hawaii, Sir." He said, "Oh, you're one of them Foreign Exchange pilots….."

Mr. Graham, who was the CEO of Graham Aviation, was the Southeast US Badminton Champion for years. He heard that I was a badminton player.

My NYU professor, who like Mr. Graham, was a world-class player and I learned the game in New York. I had the opportunity to play against the world champions from Thailand who worked out at the McBirnie YMCA in Manhattan where I worked. To play the world's best was another great once in a lifetime experience for this kid from Palolo Avenue, Honolulu, Hawaii.

So often when I wasn't on the flying schedule, I would be called to play badminton with Mr. Graham. My flying classmates claimed that it was how I got through Primary Pilot Training.

Much later, in the early nineties, I drove my family from our home in Niceville, FL to Marianna to revisit the Primary Pilot Training site. Graham Air Base is now called Marianna Municipal Airport. A guard greeted us at the gate entrance, and I told him that I was a graduate of this facility. He looked at me rather puzzled, and we found out why. There was a sign that read: "Welcome to the State of Florida – Institution for Mental Rehabilitation." It nevertheless, was a nostalgic tour of the base. Some of the old brick buildings were still there.

Such great memories.

BASIC PILOT TRAINING -- BIG SPRING, TEXAS

Following Primary Pilot Training, we were transferred to Basic Jet Flight Training at Webb AFB TX, where I flew first in the newer T-28 trainer followed by my first exposure to a jet aircraft called the T-33A. (Jan-June 1956)

T-28

T-33A Jet PilotTrainer in the fifties

A Controlled Crash in a West Texas Cotton Patch -- Class 56-Q--Webb AFB TX -- January '56.

My transition into the T-28 went very well with one exception. The T-28 engine quit on one of my early pre-solo transition flights flying with instructor, 2/Lt Jeff Vanderwalk. I was practicing a cloverleaf, and as we were inverted, oil poured out of the exhaust. Jeff took over and rolled the aircraft level and called on the radio, "may-day, engine quit south of Stanton." The two-bladed prop seized horizontally. We were flying at 3,000 feet above the ground with no power, and Lt. Vanderwalk set up a glide according to procedures. A decision had to be made to bail out the side, or set up a forced landing pattern and select a flat piece of terrain to put the crippled aircraft.

I opened the canopy according to forced landing procedures. As there were nothing but cotton patches over the flat land of West Texas, it was an easy decision for Jeff to select a recently plowed field for landing. After flying in a circular text-book forced landing pattern, Jeff almost routinely belly-landed the T-28 with the wheels up skidding 75 feet in the center of the selected cotton patch. The rapid deceleration caused my head-set to slip off my head and slam hard into the windshield.

Super piloting by my IP, 2/Lt Vanderwalk.

We quickly vacated the aircraft, and noticed that there was a man plowing the perimeter of the same cotton patch. There was a small white dog with a black spot on his side, running along the plow. It was a Mexican itinerant farmer, who continued to plow. When I finally waved him down, he stopped the plow and shouted, "Are you having any trouble?"

His question cracked us up as we pointed to the aircraft flat on its belly in the middle of the Cotton patch still emitting black smoke.

Soon after, an aircraft flew low to check on us. It was flight commander, Capt Carl Sprague, we waved, and fire trucks and an ambulance appeared, followed by a crane and a flat bed truck. An Air Force engineer and a lawyer appeared and made arrangements with the landowner to compensate her for "damaging" her cotton patch. It seems the team had done this before, many times. Ours wasn't the first T-28 to have engine metal chips in the oil system.

Jeff Vanderwalk and I were deemed healthy by the attending flight surgeon, and I asked his medic to radio-relay a message to my wife that everything was ok. (no cell phones, of course)

It was routine after that.

The aircraft was transported on a flatbed to the base, and after they dropped the landing gear, they replaced the engine and damaged belly panels, and the aircraft flew again in a few weeks.

Instructor Vanderwalk was commended for his airmanship. I haven't seen Jeff since then. Great guy.

There was nothing in the local media about our gear-up landing in Stanton, TX. No CNN.

I graduated ranking 7th in my pilot training class of 72, and I thought that I was eligible to request a coveted tactical fighter training assignment at Williams AFB, AZ. However, I was extremely disappointed when the Air Training Command directed that the top ten from each pilot training class be held back in the Training Command to become T-33 basic training instructors. I wanted so much to be a fighter pilot, but my supervisors advised me to be patient, and that I would eventually be assigned to fighters.

So after attending Basic Pilot Instructor School for three months in Selma, Alabama, I returned as a full-fledge Instructor Pilot (IP).

I had just been promoted to first lieutenant, and was assigned my first four students from Class 57-O.

1st Lt. Kan and his first four 2nd Lt students:
Tom Rush, Warren Sams, Joe Lucas and Tony Ross.

<u>Tragedy on my first full day of work as an instructor,</u> (in late September '56)

My flight commander, Capt. Carl Sprague, asked me to go out with him to the mobile control vehicle to observe the night training operations involving students and instructors from two flights. Flight commanders took turns controlling night flying operations from the mobile control situated near the takeoff end of the runway. As it got dark, there was a stream of T-33s taxiing out for takeoff.

They all had their navigation lights on and were cleared to take off one by one by Capt Sprague, who had complete control of one of two runways. After fifteen or so aircraft took off it would be 20 minutes or so before the aircraft would return to base for practice night landings. When a student demonstrated three successful landing attempts, he would be deemed qualified and cleared by the instructor for night solo flights.

During that 20-minute lull, a strange thing happened.

We saw an unlit aircraft in the dim moonlight, taxiing toward the departure end of the runway. Capt. Sprague called, "aircraft on taxiway one, turn your navigation lights on and identify yourself."

The lights came on, but there was no radio reply. Without clearance, the aircraft took the runway, powered up, and started its takeoff roll. Capt. Sprague called "Aircraft on takeoff roll, Abort your takeoff. Abort. Abort!" to no avail. Sprague got on the phone and called base operations.

The aircraft got airborne unsteadily, and it climbed slowly.

Then a distressed Airdrome Officer on duty at base operations reported that an airman (enlisted) crew chief was in that aircraft alone.

He started the aircraft on his own, and he was sitting on the crew chief cushion with no parachute.

We watched the aircraft with its lights on turning to the east toward the city of Big Spring, climbing slowly.

Then the airman with his crew chief headset on called. "Hello this is Airman _____. I'm sorry to cause all of this trouble."

Capt. Sprague: "Do you have any flying experience?"

Airman: "I have a few hours in the flight simulator."

Capt. Sprague: "What is your altitude and your airspeed?"

Airman: "I think I'm at two-thousand feet and the airspeed is one-hundred-forty."

Capt. Sprague: "Do you have the landing gear up and flaps up."

Airman: "I raised the landing gear." (He took off with the flaps up.)

Capt. Sprague: "Increase your RPM with the throttle to 90% and push the trim button down until you get a trim neutral green light." (Crew chiefs are familiar with those terms.)

Capt. Sprague was trying to get the airman to attain a safe airspeed and to maintain level flight, but chances of saving this non-pilot without a parachute was almost nil.

All of a sudden we saw the aircraft plummet straight down and then a flash when it hit the ground. The aircraft hit southeast of Big Spring in an open field, about two miles from the Cosden Oil Refinery. We could only speculate on why he suddenly dove and crash. He could have lost control or his dive could have been suicidal. The rumor that the airman was aiming the aircraft at the oil refinery was quickly squelched.

It was revealed that he had a history of mental disturbance, and on that evening, he was directed to work when he thought it was his night off and was disgruntled.

It was already the second fatality I witnessed first hand in my short Air Force career and it wouldn't be the last.

The Webb Air Force Base Public Relations office released the news as a "pilot training" accident and kept the suicide aspect out of the news media to preclude public panic and uproar.

Today such news could not be concealed from the press and TV. There was no such thing then as "network" distribution. Local news release: "there was an accident; name of the deceased is withheld until notification of next of kin," appeared in the media, period.

Because the community in the city of Big Spring, Texas was accustomed to seeing an occasional aircraft crash, they didn't pay much attention to this accident. (It was just 6 months before, that we crash-landed in the T-28 in a nearby cotton patch and there was nothing in the morning paper about it.)

In a week, it seemed everyone erased that incident from his or her minds and it was business as usual. Incredible.

As a matter of fact, when I got shot down in Southeast Asia in 1965, there was nothing in the Honolulu papers about it. Except for immediate families, no one seemed to care about any of the 47,378 killed in action in Vietnam.

Media indifference turned out to be a blessing for me because neither wife Nan nor my Mom learned about my being shot down. Nan found out about it later and I never told my Mom I was in combat. (She might have suspected) Today if a Hawaii born pilot got shot down over Iraq, could you imagine the coverage on the local TV and in the Honolulu Star Bulletin and Advertiser?

FINALLY, KAN IS A FIGHTER PILOT!
F-84F ' --- F4B/C

It took six years of lobbying through official as well as informal channels to become a fighter pilot. I became an F4C Phantom pilot after two years of training in the single-seat F-84F. Part of that "training" came standing on alert to attack Cuba during the '63 Cuban Crisis at MacDill AFB, Tampa, FL. The previous years as a "Training Commando" gave me overall flying experience, but no where is piloting as demanding (or as thrilling) as in everyday tactical fighter flying.

Before Vietnam in the early sixties, the US discovered that Cuba was installing intercontinental nuclear missiles provided by the Soviet Union. The Cuban crisis ensued. I was assigned to the 12th Tactical Fighter Wing, MacDill AFB, Tampa FL, flying the antiquated Korean War vintage F84F. We were put on alert to attack Cuba and my assigned target was an SA-2 radar van on San Antonio Delos Banos Airfield located on the extreme western tip of Cuba. That target was at a distance that would try the maximum range of the F-84F. Given ideal conditions, we calculated that we would return with minimum fuel. We were ridiculously and anemically armed with two napalm bombs and a few hundred .50 cal rounds. Our target was well equipped to shoot us down with Russian supplied modern radar aided antiaircraft artillery (AAA) as well as SA-2 ground to air guided missiles. (The same missile that shot me down in Vietnam a couple of years later.) The USAF was so poorly equipped. We had old Korean War technology in our jet fighters.

I was so relieved that Russia backed off and JFK called the alert off as I figured I would never have survived that mission.

<u>Small World Side Story</u>: In the early '90s after I had returned to FL from my five years with McDonnell-Douglas-Korea, I worked for TASC/

Litton as a consultant in Fort Walton Beach. I became acquainted with Abel Fernandez, a Cuban-naturalized American Civil Engineer who as a young man defected from Cuba with his family on a boat. I found out through casual conversation that he grew up in San Antonio Delos Banos, Cuba. When asked, Abel said he remembered seeing the SA-2 installation through the perimeter fence at the airport, and there was a radar antenna on the van (fan-song radar). He recalled that there were SA-2 missile sites close by, and numerous MIG-21 aircraft on the ramp. I could only surmise that he was describing our Cuban crisis target objective. Again, I'm glad we weren't launched in our antiquated fighters. We would not have been a match against the MIGs and SA-2 missiles.

Out of the F-84F and into the AF's First Team:

In the spring of '63, I finally got the premier fighter assignment with the first squadron to acquire USAF's newly acquired fighter, the F4C Phantom II. Before the F4Cs were delivered to the 12th Fighter Wing at MacDill AFB, we were trained in borrowed US Navy F4Bs (with USAF markings.) After three months of intensive upgrade training, we were deemed "combat ready" in the versatile F4 including qualification in nuclear weapons delivery.

A handful of us were transferred to Eglin AFB in Northwest Florida with eight new F4C aircraft to test and certify a variety of weapons and tactics for use on the F4C. It was a wonderful fighter flying assignment. We performed tests on various runway arresting barriers; conducted numerous short-field landing tests with McAir test pilots; conducted comprehensive weapons firing and release tests called "Seek Eagle Verification; fired and dropped a variety of weapons on firepower demonstrations including maximum load bombs and rockets and simulated nuclear weapons. Many demonstrations at night under flares; three gun pod simultaneous firings demonstrations; Mach 2.2

(over twice the speed of sound) energy maneuverability performance verification flights; laser-ranging bomb computer tests, deployments to Army installations to demonstrate our tactical capabilities; etc. With each of us flying twice a day in a variety of weapons and tactical tests, the eight assigned pilots of Det #1 557ᵗʰ TFS at Eglin AFB became uniquely experienced pilots in the US Air Force's newest fighter.

An example of a "unique" test mission:

One test day, I was scheduled to fly an "intercept" mission on an unnamed target. On that day, my back-seater was a pilot named Walt Wurzbach, who was a former radar intercept officer and considered one of the best on air defense air-to-air radar. A mysterious team from higher headquarters briefed us somewhat vaguely on our mission.

Our mission profile was simply, takeoff, head south into the Gulf of Mexico and under the guidance of a ground based intercept radar site, search and find their designated target on our radar, and perform an intercept simulating a radar missile firing and "kill" the target.

Walt and I wondered what was so difficult about that? The F-4 had the best air-to-air intercept radar, capable of detecting large targets over 150 miles away, locking on at 50 miles. When the radar locks on, there was a magic circle on the radarscope, and as long as I kept the target (a dot) within the circle, we were in proper intercept parameters. When the circle enlarged, it indicated that I was in range and it was the signal to launch the missile(s). The F-4, along with the AF F-106 was the best air defense fighters of that era.

The mystery team never told us what our target was, and only instructed us to intercept and achieve a radar "kill."

So on cue, we took off to the South toward the Gulf of Mexico, performing a maximum climb on a heading of 180 degrees (South) to

35,000 in afterburner, which took less than three minutes. The radar site said our target was to our right at 60 degrees at 80 miles. Walt immediately located the target, and he remarked that it was well above us. So I climbed to 40,000 and accelerated to 1.5 Mach (supersonic).

At about 45 miles Walt locked on to the target, and the radar computer indicated that I had to make a hard left turn to keep the "dot" in the circle. Walt said it looked like the target was some 20,000 feet above us and traveling faster than Mach 2. I pulled the aircraft into a tight turn in order to maintain the proper intercept angle. As hard as I turned, I couldn't keep our target in our magic circle. We rolled out behind, in trail of the target, way out of firing range. The target was pulling away from us and we were flying at 1.5 Mach. (about 1200 mph). The radar site called off the intercept and when we landed, the briefing team was gone, and we heard nothing about the mission from anyone. It was Top Secret.

The "target" we found out much later was an SR-71, and in 1964 a deep dark military secret.

We finally figured out that the boys from the Pentagon wanted to find out if the Mach 2 F4C Phantom could intercept the Mach 3 SR-71, and apparently they were satisfied and happy that it couldn't.

At three times the speed of Sound and flying at over 70,000, it was impossible for the Phantom or any Soviet fighter to intercept the Blackbird.

Mission: Energy Maneuverability (EM) test flight at Mach 2.2. Spring of 1964

I was tasked to attain over twice the speed of sound at 38,000 feet and at level flight turn the aircraft as hard as it will turn. Radar and photo-theodolite filming was used to record the flight performance. The arrogant genius, Maj John Boyd, was verifying his

Energy Maneuverability (EM) Theory, comparing the F4 Phantom performance mathematically with his computer assessment of Soviet aircraft performance based on design and power. My Weapons System Officer (F4 pilot backseater) was Capt. Bob Stone.

A tragic day—I should have been killed

I had just started up, pre-taxi checks completed, and about to taxi when Ops Officer Major Bob Brockmann approached the aircraft signaling me to shut down. He beckoned me out of the aircraft.

There was a change. I was directed to fly another aircraft that urgently required a test device to be installed at MacDill AFB near Tampa.

There was a Command regulation specifying that only instructor pilots (IPs) were allowed to fly in the F4 alone, and there wasn't anyone available to fly in the back seat. So Capt. Mike Lesicko, our flying safety officer, not an IP, was assigned to take my place in the EM Test mission with Bob Stone.

Mike appeared in his G-suit and gear and he climbed into that cockpit as I started up the other aircraft to fly to MacDill AFB by myself.

Bob Brockmann had already filed a flight plan for my flight to Tampa. I taxied out ahead of Mike & Bob and took off on my coastline low-level flight to MacDill. It would be a fun, relaxing flight for me and Mike Lesicko would enjoy the Mach 2 flight, I thought.

When I arrived less than an hour later at MacDill, I checked in with Maj Brockmann.

To my great dismay, Maj Brockmann said, "Mike Lesicko was killed in an inadvertent (seat) ejection taxiing out for takeoff. It happened just after you left, Bob."

It was a freak accident. The F4 Phantom has two cockpit canopies that raised and lowered independently. In those early days, the ejection seat propulsion was via a 40mm cannon shell, and an aircrew could not survive an ejection from ground zero. Today, the seats are equipped with rocket propulsion and an aircrew can be ejected at zero altitude, zero airspeed.

Each canopy has a shaft that raised and lowered the canopy. This shaft had a shear pin that was designed to break when the aircrew pulled his ejection handles to allow the canopy to release free of the aircraft.

But this shear pin is not supposed to break on ordinary raising and lowering of the canopy.

Bob Stone, my co-pilot routinely lowered his rear canopy as they were taxiing out for takeoff. When Mike in the front seat lowered his, the canopy came down, the shear pin broke and the shaft detached from the canopy. The shaft was then leaning precariously against the ejection mechanism of Mike's ejection seat.

Bob Stone shouted, "Don't recycle!!!" …. but as any fighter pilot would, when Mike saw the "canopy unlocked" light on, he immediately recycled before Bob's warning, which started the canopy shaft moving into the "banana links" and it fired the seat.

Mike was ejected through the heavy hard plastic canopy and he landed on the tail of the aircraft. He died of severe internal injuries in the ambulance on the way to the hospital. A one in a billion accident.

All of this went on as I was merrily flying along the Big Bend of the Florida Gulf Coast line.

It was excruciatingly painful for me, as had the crew change had not occurred I definitely would have recycled the canopy as Mike did and I would've been killed.

It was so very hurtful at Mike's funeral. Maurene Lesicko was so gracious. I felt so guilty.

It should've been me!

Capt. Mike Lesicko, father of four.

SUMMER 1964

Following the dismantling of the 4485th Tactical Warfare Center (TAWC) Test Wing at Eglin AFB, the seven F4C pilots from TAWC were transferred to the newly formed 33rd Fighter Wing on the other side of the vast Eglin airfield. As we were all experienced F4 pilots, we were assigned as Instructor Pilots (IP). I was assigned as the personal instructor pilot for the Wing Commander, Col. David C. Jones, who later became the Chief of Staff of the Air Force and Chairman, Joint Chiefs.

One of the routine tasks for the IP was to assist in the supervision of training of the new pilots in the 33rd wing. We were called "Airdrome Officers."

We instructors routinely monitored landings from a small mobile control unit sitting at the approach end of the runway.

While I was on duty in the mobile unit one day, an F-104 pilot returning from a test mission declared an emergency because the right main gear was stuck in the retracted position. His left landing gear and nose gear were down and locked. He flew by for a visual check. It was a two-seater F-104, two pilots on board.

After the aircrew and their operations officer on the ground exhausted all possible ways of unlocking the right gear, and they were getting low on fuel, it was decided that a landing would be attempted with the two of three gears down.

The runway was foamed to preclude fire caused by the sparks and friction when the right wing came in contact with the runway.

The F-104 was cleared to land to the northwest on runway 32. The pilot made a nice landing and rolled upright until the airspeed diminished and the right wing dropped and the wingtip fuel tank came in contact with the runway. The tank bounced off of the runway and the aircraft tipped to the left and the left tip tank hit the runway, bouncing it back to the right.

Apparently the pilot in the rear seat thought that the aircraft would roll over so he ejected at ground level. I believe the aircraft had sequential ejection seats so the front seat pilot was involuntarily ejected soon after.

The pilots landed and were killed as they hit the runway, the chutes never did open. Rocket propelled ejection seats had not been invented yet. Rocket seats would have saved their lives.

The sadly ironic part of it all was the aircraft came to a stop off the runway upright and had the pilots stayed in the aircraft they would've most likely survived.

Soon after I left Eglin to join the 433rd at Ubon AB Thailand.

Next: Chapter 9 – Vietnam

CHAPTER 9

VIETNAM -- THAILAND

VIETNAM WAR DAYS

December 16, 1965

When I joined the 433rd Fighter Squadron which deployed to Ubon Thailand from George AFB, CA, (Dec '65) we all, to the man suffered acutely from dysentery, better known as the "runs." It was so bad that during our pre-combat indoctrination briefings, guys were soiling their flight suits left and right without any warning and without time to make it to the latrine.

So our flight surgeon asked each aircrew to provide stool samples in a cup. I thought it a waste of time, since everyone had the same problem; all he needed was a cross-section of a few samples.

No, the Doctor wanted all to provide samples.

So I took my co-pilot Joe Moran, whom I had just met, into the neighboring rice field. We crawled through the barbed wire and scooped up water buffalo dung, and turned the cups in. Next day, the flight surgeon happily announced they had isolated and solved the problem... Turns out that the Officers' Club dining hall wasn't washing the vegetables properly....

"and by the way," the doctor said in mock-seriousness, "there are two aircrew member who are eating too much grass."

Note: In those days, the public water anywhere in Thailand was not very pure, so when we went downtown, we refrained from drinking water. Since there was no bottled water, we just drank beer at the local restaurants. The flight surgeon took the trouble to show us the local water that the indigenous folks drank under a microscope. It was like what we saw in our ninth grade science class. Lots of little guys crawling around. Paramecium, amoeba, etc., which is probably why at that time the Thai longevity was a mere 47 years of age.

**The 433rd Fighter Squadron – Satan's Angels –
Ubon AB, Thailand - Jan '66**

Vietnam Air Combat:

Recently I have searched for names of fighter pilots born in Hawaii who flew combat in the Vietnam War early on. There is little information available. Thus far, I only know of only four others.

1. <u>Col. Paul Kunichika.</u> Paul had an outstanding reputation at the AF Fighter Weapons Center at Nellis AFB, Nevada. Flew the F-105 into North Vietnam from Korat AB, Thailand. I believe Paul flew with the Hawaii Air National Guard as well.

2. <u>Commander Cliff Wakatake,</u> a USN pilot who flew A-6 Intruders off of carriers in Vietnam.

3. <u>Capt or Major VernRoy Ahnin,</u> flew F-100s in South Vietnam.

4. <u>Brigadier General Dwight Kealoha;</u> flew RF-4C reconnaissance "unarmed and unafraid" on two combat tours. He later flew F4Ds and A-10s.

5. <u>...</u>and Me.

A well known Japanese-American (JA) pilot hero is California born USN Capt (ret) Gordon Nakagawa, who flew the A-6B from a carrier. He was shot down in October '72 in N Vietnam and was captured and imprisoned in Hanoi for the duration of the war.

I recently discovered that another JA, Col (ret) Terry Ueyama was a RF4C reconnaissance pilot who spent five years as a POW in Hanoi. ('68-'73).

SA-2 MISSILE SHOOTS US DOWN

In 1965, North Vietnam, with the help of the Russian and Chinese technicians, installed SA-2 Surface to Air Missile Systems (SAMS), 100mm, 57mm and 37mm AAA guns, and perhaps began testing of prototype shoulder-mounted SA-9's (like US Army's Redeye & Stinger). We were flying our Mach 2 Phantoms equipped with 1945

World War II avionics and armament. We had no up to date electronic countermeasure (ECM) protection, no bombing computer systems, and no guided bombs.

On that mission we got shot down by an SA-2 missile, we were on a MIG-cap mission, which means we were assigned to fly protective escort over our F-105 fighter bombers, to shield them from North Vietnam MIG fighters while they attempted to destroy the highly defended Cao Nung Bridge on the Northeast Railroad line to China with unguided "dumb" bombs. Because we didn't have the sophisticated stand-off guided bombs of today, the F-105 bombers had to get down dangerously close to the targets and they were sitting ducks for the North Vietnamese gunners. The U.S. lost a total of 282 F-105s and 193 F-4s (we were the 11th) in North Vietnam combat (not including operational losses or South Vietnamese casualties) …Can you imagine the outrage today if we lost that many in Iraq? …but no one seemed to care then.

Our call sign was "Buick 2," number two in a flight of four, being led by a major who had no tactical fighter experience. He was leading only because he was a major and the rest of us were captains and lieutenants. The takeoff, refueling and fighter escort to the target went well. The F-105 flight dropped their bombs without hitting the bridge. The anti-aircraft defense was fierce, and one F-105 was hit, and we heard the pilot say that he was bailing out and "I'll see you after the war." They were so brave.

After we completed our MIG cap mission, our flight leader headed south to return to home base. He got disoriented and we wandered into a "SAM ring." We made frantic calls to tell the leader that we were on the wrong course, but he told us to shut up. We ended up directly over the dangerous areas that we were briefed by Intelligence to avoid. You can imagine the delight of the North Vietnamese (and Russian) missile crews when they saw a flight of US fighters within their operational parameters. If it weren't so cloudy, we might have had a chance to dodge the SAMs visually.

Neither Joe Moran, nor I "saw" the SAMs coming up through the clouds over the vicinity of Hanoi. I was "jinking," making hard turns randomly left and right to avoid the heavy AAA bursting around us. As the 30 foot SA-2 missile passed close to us it was command-detonated from the ground and hundreds of fragments hit the bottom of our aircraft. We luckily didn't suffer a direct hit. We would've been blown to bits by the thirty-foot missile. As we flipped over from the blast, two more SAMs whizzed by. Our right engine was killed immediately and the left engine coughed and was slowly losing power.

Seeing the fire warning and engine overheat lights, Joe said, "We're on fire, we better get out." We were still over heavily populated territory, so I told Joe to hang on. I attempted air starts on the "good" engine" by pushing on the ignition button and jockeying the throttle. After three or so failed air-start attempts, I decided to push the throttle up into the full after-burner (AB) position. We would either blow up or if the AB lit, we would be able to get out of the populated area. My guardian angel was still with us. IT LIT!, and the crippled aircraft gained speed and climbed. The powerful thrust was orgasmic, a real kick in the ass. As we gained altitude, the little fire in the aft section must have extinguished from lack of oxygen.

In the confusion, we lost the flight leader (or he lost us) and we never saw or heard from our leader again. Buick 3 and Buick 4 searched and found us after the SAM break-up. Buick 4, piloted by my good friend Don King (a few months later killed in action), flew up to my aircraft and observed that we had a small fire in the aft section, and recommended that I jettison our three fuel tanks and eight air-to-air missiles, which I did. One of my AIM-7 missiles got hung-up and hit the aircraft tail section and curled up the horizontal stabilator, but luckily it did not affect the control of the aircraft. According to Don King our aircraft was full of triangular holes from the SAM fragments and fuel was leaking profusely through those holes. Because I had to jettison the external fuel tanks, we were already down to "bingo" (better land now) fuel level. Buick 3, Jack Walker, called for a refueling tanker, but that idea was squelched because I didn't have the hydraulic pressure to open the refueling receptacle. So the best we could do was to continue to fly south over the mountains of Northern Laos away from the bad guys.

We flew for about 20 minutes in minimum (stage-one) afterburner, which put us well South when the "good engine" finally flamed out as the fuel tank read zero. It occurred to me that it is rare for any fighter pilot to see zero on his fuel gauge when airborne. The F4C had an emergency ram-air-turbine (RAT) that I extended, which provided some hydraulic pressure for controls and electrical power to communicate after the flameout. We were in Laos. Joe said something like, "See you on the ground!" and ejected at 10,000 feet,

It was strangely quiet. Because I still had control of the aircraft, I guided the aircraft away from a farm village in the distance, then ejected. Everything in the complicated Martin-Baker ejection seat worked beautifully, except the inflated raft broke away from the end of the survival kit tether. Later I thought of the incongruity, when perhaps a farmer below found the inflated one-man raft in his vegetable garden. I saw the aircraft hit the ground. With no fuel it didn't explode. It just plunged in a steep dive into the soft soil and seemed to disappear.

I inflated my LPU (life preserver unit) as I anticipated being banged about through the dry trees below. The early F4C ejection systems had the US Navy 28 foot diameter parachutes, and the rate of descent was considerably faster than that of the US Air Force's 36-foot chutes. I was bounced around the branches and I hit the ground pretty hard. Joe said he also hit the ground pretty hard. I gathered up my parachute, put the survival items in my pocket and hid everything I didn't need in a bush. I must say at this point that the Air Force survival training I had was outstanding. Everything I was taught, from ejection, parachute landing falls and survival was applied to the maximum.

I heard Joe talking on the radio to someone. Because he bailed out from a much higher altitude than I, he was still on his way down. Joe landed in the next valley. My guardian angel was STILL present. It was around 4:00 P.M. and as luck would have it, there were "Jolly Green" rescue CH-3 helicopters in the vicinity on their way home after picking up F-105 crews who were shot down in the morning missions.

When one of the CH-3 rescue choppers in the area heard me on the radio, (we each had two small emergency radios), they headed my way, hovered some fifty feet above me and dropped the rescue anchor to pick me up...I have been saved, <u>I thought.</u>

Before the rescue anchor got to me, they suddenly pulled the line up and flew off in a hurry. I got on the radio and in no uncertain words said, "where the f--k are you guys going?" They came back and picked me up. As I climbed into the chopper, I saw that the pilot was Capt Barry Kamhoot, whom I knew at Eglin AFB. I asked, "Why the hell did you leave me?" Barry said "well, as my para-medic was dropping the line, he got a good look at you, and thought you were a Vietnamese (I didn't look like a real American) and he perceived it as a trap. He pressed the panic button. So I had to get out in a hurry."

"So why'd you come back?" I asked. He replied he recognized my voice (as well what was called "creative profanity."). Later on, Barry joked, "Well, the real reason we came back was because we realized that there was no such thing as a fat Vietnamese!" I wasn't fat.

Joe landed among some Thai or Laotian farmers, and Joe contemplated pulling his gun out not knowing whether or not they were friendly. They kept their distance from Joe as he was rescued.

Note: The F-105 pilots and the Jolly Green rescue crews were so courageous, they are purported to have guts of steel and balls of brass. We bought cases of Beefeater's and Johnny Walker Black for our rescuers.

The old ejection seats used a 40mm cannon shell to punch the aircrew out of the aircraft at 18 instant positive G's. Later, the seat was modified with rockets and the acceleration was gradual. I tell everyone I used to be 6 ft 4 inches tall, but now I am 5 ft 9 because of the spinal compression(s).

A SURPRISE AWAITING US AT HOME BASE

The choppers dropped us off at the northern-most USAF Thai base at Udorn Thani where we went through X-Ray and medical exams. We were then flown by C-47 "Goony Bird" back to Ubon.

Upon arrival we were shocked as we disembarked from the C-47. We were greeted by Bob Hope, whose USO show just happened to be at Ubon on Dec 19, '65. We were invited backstage (after "you guys get cleaned up," said Mr. Hope). Joe and I talked at length with Bob Hope back-stage and got to meet Jerry Colona, Anita Bryant and Joey Heatherton. Anita was truly the Orange juice lady and Joey was absolutely sensational.

Joey Heatherton and Bob Hope
We got the VIP treatment. What a day it was.

Next Day:

Our leaders recommended that Joe and I go down to Bangkok for some Rest & Relaxation (R&R), but we refused and volunteered to fly the very next day. This time we were led by a very competent flight leader, Major "Rags" Ragland on the very same mission up to the northeast railroad near Hanoi, and everything went like clockwork. Subsequently, I led all of our combat flights. The reader may wonder why the US Air Force was sending newly arrived crews on the most dangerous missions on their first two flights. It was not common practice for the USAF to do so, but they had no choice, we were all "rookies".

Unfortunately, we sadly lost "Rags"on a night mission a few months later near the coastal city of Than Hoa.

Quite an Introduction: Incidentally, that Dec 19th flight was not only our very first combat mission, but it was our very first flight together. Joe remarked that after that first flight, he still wasn't sure if I could land the aircraft safely.

On each Dec 19th, our survival anniversary, Joe and I call each other to celebrate our good fortune. We have called every year since we returned from SEA in '66.

WITH JOE MORAN
DEC 19, 1965

Joe took good care of me for the next 167 combat missions. Unless our assigned target was not in heavily defended areas, he made sure we didn't wander into the SA-2 "SAM rings." Most of sorties were at night. Because Joe flew some missions with others, he had his required 100 North Viet Nam missions before I did. He didn't have to fly any more combat missions. 100 North was the ticket to go home.

When we were initially united after our bailout, Joe gave me a big hug and said, "Only 99 to go!" Combat missions in Laos didn't count, although some of the North Laos missions were just as hazardous.

However, Joe volunteered to fly two more missions with me into North Vietnam to make sure I would complete my 100th in NVN safely. He should've gotten the Medal of Honor for that, risking his neck just to make sure I got my ticket to go home.

What a guy!

WHY WE CAN'T WIN WARS

The real enemies in WW I and WW II were clearly defined and eliminated.

In all of our conflicts since WWII, our adversaries have been surrogate enemies, nations, religious factions and even tribes, aided and hand-fed by China, Russia, Iran, Syria, etc., to forward their own national objectives and/or to weaken the mighty USA. All of the wars and skirmishes against second echelon foes have been highly political, frustrating and unwinnable. Further, since the World Wars, our strategies and tactics have been dictated by politicians in Washington, and not by our experienced military leaders. These militarily inept politicians severely handcuff the military forces, and thus, to the world our military appears disorganized and weak. The lack of progress and a clearly defined objective turned the American public against the Vietnam effort.

President Lyndon B. Johnson severely restricted us from using our full potential. However, in spite of political handicaps, and contrary to public opinion, the US forces NEVER lost a battle, air or ground, in Vietnam.

Way back in '66 we fighter pilots thought that if we were allowed to unleash our full potential, we could have, should have, obliterated North Vietnam in six months. As it was, we were not allowed to bomb the strategic targets and we never were allowed to really hurt North

Vietnam. We were only supposed to "scare" them into keeping their hands off of South Vietnam. Our only real targets were bridges, truck convoys, truck parks and one oil refinery. Much later, President Nixon tasked our B-52s to bomb Hanoi which scared them into a cease fire. Of course, after the US pulled out, the North easily took over South Vietnam.

Among our squadron mates, there were seven aircraft shot down with four fatalities and eight pilots endured seven years of hardship and torture in the Hanoi "Hilton" Prison.

Joe Moran and I were the only two rescued after being shot down in North Vietnam, and it was only because the rescue helicopters by chance were in the vicinity. Lucky.

LOST A GOOD FRIEND

About a month in theater, the 433rd squadron was assigned a night armed reconnaissance role. We flew in pairs, lights out, in a loose radar-trail formation. The #2 aircraft flew aft and to the side always with the lead in radar contact. Joe and I flew at night as flight leader for the rest of our tour. In May '66 on a road reconnaissance mission, my very good friend Don King and his co-pilot, Frank Ralston, flying in the #2 position, disappeared from the formation along the shores of southern North Vietnam. There were no distress radio calls to the flight leader Bob Hutten and there was no evidence of enemy fire or a crash. No sightings in search and rescue operations.

Later, in my research at Pacific Forces Headquarters in Hawaii, I found some intelligence reports that stated that the Russians might have been development testing their shoulder mounted ground to air missile (like our Redeye) in Vietnam. There is that possibility that Don and Frank were downed by such a missile, flying at 4,000 feet within the Redeye range.

Our pilots did report rockets being fired at us at night, but we thought they were harmless unguided 2.75 inch rockets.

In the year 2007 there is very little information from the N Vietnamese government regarding Don and Frank. The USAF POW/ MIA office has nothing.

I have maintained contact with Don's wife, Ginny and their four children.

WELCOME HOME?

When we returned home in July '66, we were ordered to wear civilian clothes upon arrival so the protesters couldn't identify us at the airport to spit on us.

University of Hawaii's protesting students were doing just that at Honolulu airport. One of my wife's nieces was a Vietnam War protester from the U of Hawaii and she asked me if I enjoyed killing innocent people. So I told her about how "innocent" those people were by relating this story:

At Ubon, Thailand, Joe and I became acquainted with a Thai educator named Uthai Phiromreun, who just returned from California, USA, with a graduate degree in education. As he spoke English so well, he agreed to be our Thai language teacher for supplemental income. The Thai government appointed him the Ubon Province District Educational commissioner.

The province farm children received no formal education before he initiated his program. He organized schools and hired teachers from Bangkok. He started with grass huts, makeshift tables and benches and a blackboard. Apparently, he was doing such an outstanding job in this remote eastern Thai province, that the Communists were alerted. The Commies did not want the Thai country folk educated. They came from Vietnam crossing Laos and the Mekong River, and found Uthai on the road. It was brutal. Uthai was found dead with bullet holes in his head. I told my wife's niece that this is the reason why I was fighting the Communists there.

However, the Jane Fonda's back home were in denial and would not listen. My niece seemed to think I was making up that "idealistic" story. There are some folks who cannot believe that some people can be so ruthless.

What a contrast between our homecoming from Vietnam compared to the reception our Iraq returnees are experiencing. As far as us Vietnam veterans are concerned we see no difference in our dedication to our country. We were doing our job as ordered, and then as a reward we were spat on, while those who return today are applauded, much of the time by WW II, Korea and VN vets.

47,378 of our servicemen lost their lives in combat in Vietnam.

A POST SCRIPT:

Sen. John McCain was not the only member of our Congress who was a Vietnam hero, and Prisoner of War. Two of our squadron jocks who were captured after being shot down in North Vietnam came home and became outstanding U. S. Congressman.

On February 16, 2007, Rep (R) Sam Johnson, Dallas,Texas, spoke to the House of Representatives on behalf of our Armed Forces in Iraq.

In the spring of '66, Major Sam Johnson was our Operations Officer in the 433rd Fighter Sq. at Ubon, Thailand when he was shot down and taken to the Hanoi Hilton along with his co-pilot Lt. Larry Chesley, for the duration. Sam was the leader of the USAF Thunderbirds before he came to Southeast Asia. He was a dashing leader and a super fighter pilot. He wasn't with us long enough for us to get to know him very well. Sam's inspiring speech to Congress failed to reach many deaf ears.

Another congressman, a very good friend, Douglas "Pete" Peterson, was also in our squadron at Ubon, and he was shot down and spent 6 ½ tough years in the Hanoi Hilton. When he returned to his home in Marianna FL, he was elected to two terms and then was appointed as the first US Ambassador to Vietnam by President Clinton. A few years after his wife Carlotta passed away, he married a Vietnamese lady, an Australian citizen, and is happily retired and is a businessman in Australia and Thailand.

Carlotta and Capt. Pete Peterson at Eglin AFB in '64.

Pete worked very hard at getting info/data on MIAs and it was amazing to me that he could work comfortably in Hanoi, considering the past. Of, course his happy marriage to Vi made his official tour a real positive in his life.

MR. PO ALMOST GOES TO PRISON

Mr. Po was our 32 year old Thai houseboy who cared for and cleaned our "hootch" and did our laundry. For a month eight of us slept in a screened-in hut on double-decked bunk beds before our air-conditioned private rooms were constructed.

We started to fly night reconnaissance and strike missions a month after we arrived. So our life-clocks were reversed. i.e., our lunch time was at midnight, and our cocktail hours were at sunrise.

One morning, after when we returned from an especially long and arduous night mission deep into North Vietnam, we asked Mr. Po to get some ice from the nearby Officers' Club so that we could have our Beefeaters on the rocks to celebrate.

Mr. Po left, but did not return promptly as he usually did, so after we got cleaned up, we decided to go to the club. We were a frustrated because Mr. Po did not bring us the ice and we couldn't toast the fact that we all cheated death again. As we walked to the club, we spotted Mr. Po a half-block down the street with USAF Air Police and Thai policemen. Mr. Po waved at us with a "bye-bye" gesture. I said sarcastically, "good-bye, Mr. Po," as we entered the Officers' Club. While I sat at the bar, it suddenly occurred to me (I should have realized) that the "bye-bye" hand signal in the US has an opposite message in Asia. It means "please come here" like when we beckon. Po was in trouble! So I rushed to where the police were, and saw that Po was being put in a Thai Police paddy-wagon. I learned that Po was being arrested for "stealing an aluminum pitcher" from the non-commissioned-officers' (NCO) mess hall, and he was being taken to the local jail.

I pulled Po away from the police vehicle, and told the Air Police sergeant that Po was my guy, performing an errand for us pilots, and apparently because the Officers club had no ice to spare, he went to get ice from the mess hall. He routinely borrowed an aluminum pitcher from the Officers' club to carry the ice to us so he thought he could do the same at the NCO facility.

When he grabbed the pitcher from the mess hall supply shelf, one of the cooks called the cops and had Po arrested.

I took a very relieved Mr. Po back to our quarters. There were rumors that the Thai chief of Police personally shot any Thais who stole from the Americans.

Photo Mr. Po gave to me of him and his wife.
Neat Thai tie.

It's another humorous story with a cultural twist that potentially could have become a very tragic incident.

So many other stories to tell........

Next: Chapter 10 -- Japan

CHAPTER 10

JAPAN

AT FUCHU AIR BASE, TOKYO, JAPAN – 1969-72.

After three strenuous years at Headquarters, Pacific Air Forces in Honolulu during the heat of the Vietnam War, I was assigned as assistant Chief of the Fighter Training section of Headquarters, Fifth Air Force at Fuchu, Japan. Soon after I became Chief of the fighter shop.

I came to Japan with the experience of five years as an instructor pilot in the Air Training Command, five years as a tactical fighter pilot with a combat tour in Vietnam, and three years as a fighter requirements officer at a Command Headquarters.

5th Air Force Headquarters had oversight of all fighter operations in Japan, Korea and Okinawa, and was involved in the modernization of the Japanese Air Self Defense Force (JASDF).

Our office had the task of monitoring fighter training and operations. I had a staff of five outstanding fighter pilots who handled the communications and staff work routinely. The Director of Operations, Col Robbie Robertson, had a special job for me.

To replace their F-86s and F-104s, the JASDF was purchasing 6 F4D aircraft from the US, and then Mitsubishi Industries was going to produce the F4D in country. Col Robertson was contacted by the CEO of Mitsubishi Industries, Mr. Nakagawa, who wanted to speak to an F4 fighter pilot knowledgeable in requirements, modifications and flight operations. A JASDF general, Kaburagi Kempu, also requested a USAF contact.

So I met with CEO Nakagawa at the nearby Koganei Country Club, which Mitsubishi owned. Mr. Nakagawa was educated at Columbia University and spoke English with an American accent, and said he was a friend of President Eisenhower. He was pleasantly surprised that the American "F4 Fighter expert" he was meeting was a Sansei (third-generation American-Japanese). We discussed F4 matters as we played golf. Mr. Nakagawa quickly took a liking to me and asked me to join the Koganei Golf Club. I told him I was honored but on the salary of an Air Force Lt. Colonel, I couldn't possibly afford the membership fee (close to $1 mil in 1970). He said as Chairman of the golf course he would waive the membership and green fees and in addition, he would cover all of my bets. I told him that I certainly could not accept his generosity and he understood.

I was current in the F4C at Yokota Air Base, and Mr. Nakagawa and General Kaburagi arranged for me to fly to the Japanese fighter bases to introduce the F4. I also flew to the Mitsubishi Plant in Nagoya to visit with the Mitsubishi test pilots.

A 5th Air Force Photo:

In General Kempu Kaburagi's office, with my boss, Col. "Rollo" Hull.

I seldom needed an interpreter, as most of my fighter contacts were fluent in English. However, I once had a Caucasian AF Major as my interpreter, a son of a US diplomat who grew up in Japan. The Japanese senior officials were amused that I, as a third-generation American of Japanese ancestry needed a Caucasian interpreter.

I flew to Komatsu, Miyazaki and Hyakuri Air Bases to show the F4 to the JASDF. The Japanese treated me royally. They loved the opportunity to party. Hyakuri Air Base was the first installation to receive the F4 aircraft.

Japan's First F4 Squadron:
The commander of the F-104 squadron at Hyakuri Air Base (will call him Lt. Col Suzuki) and two others received upgrade and instructor training in the F4D at Davis-Monthan AFB in Tuscon AZ. Upon

return to Japan, they would train the entire unit, the first F4 squadron in Japan.

Not long after his return, Lt. Col. Suzuki was killed in an F4 crash.

As an instructor, he was demonstrating slow flight and approach to stalls to an upgrading pilot when the aircraft went into a spin. This "departure from flight" happens when the aircraft is too slow, and the airflow over the aircraft will not sustain flight. The F4 stall is insidious as it seems initially like the aircraft is still flying and controllable. To recover the nose has to be pointed down, controls have to be precisely placed and power must be increased.

The recovery requires about 15,000 feet of altitude. If the aircraft entered this stalled condition below 15,000 feet, the flight manual recommended ejection. The captain called out to Lt. Col. Suzuki that they were already below 10,000 feet above the ground. Not enough altitude to recover. Suzuki ordered the captain to eject, which he did safely. Lt. Col Suzuki did not eject.

The safety board officially concluded that Suzuki was killed due to unknown factors. However, it was quietly acknowledged that he chose to remain in the aircraft to die rather than to face the "disgrace" of a commander losing the first JASDF F4. This extreme "save face" phenomenon is not understood by Westerners.

The Lt. Colonel seemed to be a typical fighter-pilot like the rest of us. This incident made me fully aware that even now among the modern Japanese, there still lie some deeply imbedded "samurai-like" (old warrior) cultural beliefs.

The Japanese have gone on to produce their own F4Es, followed by the successful manufacture of the F-15 aircraft. My veteran McDonnell-Douglas aircraft manufacturing expert friends tell me that the Mitsubishi F-15J would readily pass any USAF inspection coming off the Mitsubishi production line.

Note: Their fighter force mission is Self Defense, but I suspect their F-15s have the basic internal wiring for an offensive air-to-ground bombing capability.

Next: Chapter 11 – Korea

CHAPTER 11

KOREA

I spent 22 interesting years with Koreans from 1969 through 1991 in five distinctly different roles:

1. 1969-72 -- Chief, Fighter Training, Headquarters 5AF, Japan. Responsible for overseeing Fighter Wing training programs at USAF bases in Japan, Okinawa and Korea. Flew the F4C out of Yokota AB, Japan; spent much time at Osan, Kunsan, Taegu Air Bases, Korea.

2. 1972-73 – Commander, 80th Fighter Squadron (F4D), Kunsan AB.

3. 1975-77 -- Chief of Plans, Programs and Foreign Military Sales, Headquarters Joint US Military Assistance Group, Yongsan Army Compound in Seoul.

4. 1978-83 – Following AF retirement, Special Assistant to CEO, Yong Jin Enterprise Co. Manama, Bahrain and Inchon, Korea.

5. 1986-91 – Managing Director, McDonnell-Douglas Korea.

First, I will be the first to admit, I still have much to learn about the Koreans. Until recent exposure to Western culture and influences, they have been the most homogenous race I have seen in my world travels.

Two thousand years of living in tight consanguinity with almost no racial intermarriage has made them so identifiable in looks and their everyday behavior, <u>almost </u>predictable.

Saving face, high respect for elders, great concern for what "others" may say or think, are very strong considerations in their everyday behavior.

Some of my observations:

1. Korean Lady Professional Golfers – one will notice that regardless of height, most of the Korean lady golfers have very strong, thick legs and forearms and wrists. I have struggled and sometimes lost in arm wrestling with several seemingly petite Korean women. They all have very similar golf swings, like they all had the same swing teacher. They are not demonstrative; their demeanor is uniform, gentle and reserved. (I'm not referring to the more loquacious Americans of Korean ancestry.)

2. Ask a middle-aged Korean man if he would like to go to lunch or dinner, he will immediately look at his watch. Until recently, Koreans have led very regimented lives and habitually ate meals at specific times; like lunch at 11:30 and dinner at 5:30.

3. Saying hello to Koreans…unless they have been in the USA for a while, they will not use your name in the salutation like Americans do. Americans delight in saying your name in salutations. Koreans will just say "Hello" omitting your name so that it would save you the embarrassment of trying to remember their names in the greeting. They will politely hand you their name cards for identification.

4. Many more unique behaviorisms. I will elaborate if you ask me.

1. 1969-72--MY FIRST EXPOSURE TO KOREA:

Before I transferred to Japan, I was allowed to get requalifed in the F4 aircraft at George AFB, CA, so that I could fly with the 80th Fighter Squadron at Yokota Air Base west of Tokyo. The 80th commander was Lt. Col. David Oakes, a good friend.

The Air Force flying community has been so good to me, I forget some of the irritating administrative errors I have endured at the hands of the uninformed support folks.

<u>Sidebar Note:</u> It was at this time at George AFB that I was fortunate to have the opportunity to fly with the Israel Air Force while I was getting recurrent and combat ready. Their pilots were flying in our F4Es engaging in mock air battles with our best pilots, and their maintenance personnel were studying the aircraft 14 hours a day, seven days a week. I befriended one of their aces, Major Avihu Ben Nun, who later as a four-star general, became the Chief of Staff, IAF. For years, before I went to work with the Arabs, I received Christmas cards from Ben. Years later I got to know the Palestinians. My feeling?…Never the twain shall meet.

As an attached pilot, I volunteered to sit on air defense alert at Osan Air Base in Korea for the 80th Squadron. I was happy to get the flying time and training. I was often "scrambled" to check out an "unknown," which usually turned out to be a foreign airliner. I once was scrambled at night over the Yellow Sea to observe ROK Air Force F-80 fighters attacking a North Korean spy boat under flares dropped by their C-119 aircraft. In the '70s, North Korean agents frequently infiltrated into South Korea using small boats. The Korean F-80s had only 30 cal machine guns. I had an immensely more powerful 20 mm gatling gun pod on board, and asked the Koreans if I could help, but US forces were prohibited to enter such forays. I know I could've obliterated the North Korean boat with one quick burst. I never found out the results of the attack.

My primary job was Chief of the Fighter Training Branch, Headquarters 5th Air Force in Tokyo.

In the early '70s the Republic of Korea Air Force (ROKAF) was starting to show signs of maturing into a world-class air force. The South Korean economy was flourishing and they were gradually acquiring state-of-the-art weapons systems. The US provided the ROKAF several squadrons of F5s gratis under the Military Assistance Program. They then purchased F4D aircraft through the Foreign Military Sales program, with plans to purchase new F-4E's down the road. The ROKAF was anxious to compare/evaluate its capability, and on one of my courtesy visits to a ROKAF fighter base, Brigadier General Kim In Ki suggested to me that we hold a gunnery meet between ROKAF and the USAF.

"Gunnery Meet" defined: A gunnery meet was a bombing and strafing (firing guns) "Top-Gun" competition, where accuracy depended on pilot skill to maneuver the aircraft in position to deliver weapons. (Before computerized weapons systems or guided weapons were installed) Up to a 140-foot bomb miss in those days was a qualifying score. Without present day computerized systems, the pilot had to compensate for wind, variations in dive angle and airspeed. With the advent of sophisticated bombing computers, GPS and laser guided bombs and missiles, these competitions are now obsolete.

I took the Gen Kim's proposal back to my Director of Operations in Japan, and he liked the idea. It took a couple of months to get organized, and the meet was funded and scheduled at the Koon-Ni gunnery range, operated by the USAF on the west coast of South Korea, 15 miles from Osan AB. Top guns from each of five squadrons from each side participated. F-105s and F4s from the US side, and F4s, F5s and F86Fs from the ROKAF.

To make a long story short, the USAF won easily. Our top guns were too good.

For diplomatic purposes I arranged for the presentation of two sets of identical trophies with first, second and third place team and individual awards to each side. A spirited awards banquet was held in Korea with lots of comradery, and all concerned were extremely satisfied.

The entire project went smoothly......EXCEPT...

EXCEPT for our helicopter flight to the gunnery range on the day of the meet.

The ROKAF co-chairman counterpart for the meet was a ROKAF Lt. Colonel, I think his name was Chun. A USAF H-19 chopper was scheduled to take us to the range 15 miles west of Osan AB to officiate from the gunnery range control tower.. We were flying for about 10 minutes just a few hundred feet above the ground to the range when we saw a yellowish fluid (hydraulic) flowing over the passenger-side windows. Simultaneously, the engine chugged and then the rotors froze and the aircraft descended rather rapidly. A catastrophic engine failure!

The aircrew was then too busy to talk to us passengers. We fell rapidly out of the sky and crashed hard on an elevated cart path that separated rice paddies and the aircraft broke in half. Our seats violently broke loose from their fastenings and Chun and I were thrown out into the center of the rice paddy. My guardian angel (again) must have been watching over us as we were plopped gently in the muddy rice paddy uninjured. Both the pilot and copilot survived but were injured. The pilot called Osan tower for help. When we gathered our wits, my

ROKAF counterpart and I decided that we would have to jog to the gunnery range, as the first fighters were due on the range in less than an hour to start the competition. After the rescue chopper and medics arrived and the aircrew attended to, Chun and I jogged the remaining two or three miles and we got there in plenty of time. We were later reprimanded (not severely) for leaving the scene of the accident. It was a Korean law.

Sidebar Note: On one of my many short tours at Osan Air Base, I met a Korean businessman named John Lee (Lee Jung Won) at the Officers' Club bar. He owned several concessions contracted to the US Air Force on three bases. He introduced himself and said he was curious in that he had never met an Asian-American Lt. Colonel before. He was doubly impressed to learn that I was a fighter pilot. I will mention him later, as he became a very close friend and a large part of my life for 25 years.

2. 1972-73--AS 80TH FIGHTER SQUADRON COMMANDER

The 80th Fighter Squadron "Headhunters" was transferred from Yokota AB Japan to Kunsan AB, Korea in '71. One of the first 80th Commanders at Kunsan was the famous Col. Solly Harp. In '71 the squadron took on a nickname, "Juvats," derived from its Latin motto, "Audentes Fortuna Juvat," or "Fortune Favors the Bold." The squadron has a rich history, originating in P-39s and P-38s in New Guinea during WW II, Richard Bong and Jay Robbins being among the top aces.

In Jan '72, the 80th Squadron Commander at Kunsan had to terminate prematurely, and the AF personnel pipeline was not ready with a replacement. As an eligible Lt. Colonel in theater, I was available, and was appointed as the replacement. It was very convenient. The 5AF Commander, who appointed me for the job, approved a waiver for my family to remain in US housing in Japan and I was subsequently able to fly to Japan on a weekends to be with them. (lucky)

It was a very exciting, most gratifying tour. I probably had the youngest fighter squadron in the Air Force with 27 first lieutenants, five captains and one major. The esprit de corps was incredible. These young fighter crews were good. They had to be proficient in aerial warfare, conventional air to ground attack and certified in nuclear weapon delivery….an immense load.

They were professional in the air and so much fun on the ground. One of my captains, Bruce "Big Fella" McClellan formed a choir, which was eventually called the "Juvat Boy's Choir." The quality and integrity of the 27 lieutenants averaging 25 years of age, assured me that we would have the world's best fighter force for years to come. It turned out to be true.

I had a super operations officer named Major Wally Armstrong, and four great captains to guide the lieutenants. I felt I had the best fighter squadron in the world and in spite of the hazardous nature of our work we were accident free.

My Wing Commander was the charismatic Col. Paul Kauttu (Brig Gen Ret), Korean/Vietnam War vet, former USAF Thunderbird, who eventually became a very good friend and golf pal.

Since the Korean War, the ROKAF had a squadron of F-86Fs at Kunsan. In '72 this squadron was co-located with our two F4D squadrons. The Korean Air Force was poorly funded. All of the Korean presidents and top leaders were former Army generals so the Army had top priority.

When I first arrived, the Korean F-86F squadron operations building was a shack with dirt floors. There was a Korean Captain Chae, their top-gun, who we called "Captain Mooch" because he used to come to our squadrons to "borrow" typing paper and anything else he could get from our office supply or personal flying equipment section. We did our best to provide our counterpart squadron with whatever we could spare. Years later, I heard some sad news that our "Capt. Mooch," Lt. Col. Chae, died in an F86F crash on take-off only a few months before they were being replaced by new F-16s.

On weekends, our squadron members would fly to Yokota Air Base in Japan in two, three or four ship formations for navigation training. Whenever I led a flight, I would show the lieutenants Mt. Fuji, which was along the route to Tokyo.

Kan at 12,000 feet circling Mt. Fuji

We had old 600-gallon centerline tanks no longer qualified to be used as fuel tanks, and our maintenance technicians cut doors and converted them to cargo carriers. Each could almost carry a disassembled motorcycle. In those days, the Yamahas and Honda bikes were still a bargain in Japan, and we carried many bikes as well as stereos and tape players back to Korea for our crews. Most of cycles were trail bikes. When it was time to return home, the aircrews would ship the bikes home or sell them to their incoming replacements.

In late summer of '72, on one of our Sunday bike excursions through the hilly trails surrounding Kunsan Air Base, we discovered an orphanage in a hidden valley. The Koreans tended to hide their orphanages. The 80th Squadron quickly adopted this orphanage of some hundred kids; they donated clothes, food, water heaters and played Santa Claus at Christmas. One of our squadron captains got his executive uncle at Montgomery Wards to donate warm winter jackets, and it was such a good feeling in the cold of Christmas Eve to see the kids put those jackets on. One of the lieutenants wanted to adopt a three year old orphan girl, but his wife at home would have nothing to do with it. He had been visiting the orphanage to see her often, and talked about adoption with the Korean officials, so it was a most tearful farewell when he was transferred.

My young aircrews were so overly enterprising raising funds for the orphanage. Once I discovered that some of the funds came from my lieutenants showing 8 mm pornography films on Saturday nights to base personnel for a $2+ donation each. (CD's were not in existence in those days) The porno flicks were obtained in Japan on our "navigation training missions." When I learned of this, I called that "committee" into my office and gave them guidance. They were to have these "shows" only at a designated building where people would attend only at their own volition and that there would not be anyone around who objected to such activity. (I unofficially had the advice and blessing of my Colonel supervisors. I even informed our squadron chaplain who rationalized "the end justified the means.")

With two months remaining on my tour, under the inspirational leadership of Wing Commander, Col. Paul Kauttu, the squadron passed an Operational Readiness Inspection with flying colors. I was so sad when Col. Kauttu told me that I "filled my square" as squadron commander, that I have earned a promotion to full colonel, and I was being moved "up" to the job of assistant wing operations officer. During this period I had time to play golf and dine with the mayor of Kunsan and to visit with friend John Lee in Seoul. I saw John throughout my tour, as he owned the Korean restaurant on base at Kunsan.

Kan -- Juvat 72

3. 1975-77 – JUSMAG-KOREA -- PLANS, PROGRAMS AND FOREIGN MILITARY SALES,

In early '73 I was informed that I had a great career progression assignment following my squadron commander tour. It was to Lakenheath AB in the UK as Assistant Wing Operations Officer of a new F4E fighter wing. It would lead to important positions after I made full colonel. While I was preparing my family to move to

England, the forming of that unit was postponed indefinitely as all of our new F4E aircraft were being diverted to Israel for their war.... a huge disappointment for me. It removed me from the fighter pilot mainstream and I was diverted to a brief tour in Electronic Warfare testing at Eglin AFB, FL. When I made full colonel, I had to again be moved and in '75 I was assigned to the Joint US Military Assistance Group in Seoul, Korea. It was a nice, benign assignment, but certainly not career enhancing. I worked for an incorrigible US Army Major General for two years. The only person who was glad I was returning to Korea was John Lee.

I worked closely with the ROK Ministry of Defense (MND), and my counterpart was an Army Colonel I will call "Col. Chung." We were responsible to arrange for the meetings between the US Secretary of Defense and the ROK Minister of Defense. I got to brief and work with Donald Rumsfeld when he was the 13th Secretary of Defense under President Gerald Ford in '75-'77.

One pleasant experience was working on an ad hoc committee for a General Robert Vessey, Commander of US Forces Korea and US 8th Army. Our job was to provide General Vessey with data to justify keeping US Forces in Korea when President Carter wanted the US to pull out of Korea. Gen Vessey's position was accepted and the troops stayed in Korea.

General Vessey told me that he became a 2/Lt. when he received a battlefield commission fighting as a sergeant alongside the heroic Japanese American 442nd infantry in Italy in WW II. A soft-spoken person, General Vessey riled senior West Point Army generals when he, a non-college graduate, was appointed Chairman of the Joint Chiefs ('82-'85). On two occasions he invited me to sit with him at dinner and he would tell me about his memorable experiences with the 442nd. A wonderful experience for me.

There are so many unusual stories to relate in my dealing with the Koreans.

One is about Colonel Chung, my ROK defense department counterpart. **It's a wild story and to the best of my knowledge true...**

(An "insider" in Korea verified the occurrences in this episode)

About a year after I met him, Chung received an assignment as the Korean Defense Attaché in the ROK embassy in Washington, D.C. I congratulated him because it was seemingly a plush assignment. Col. Chung, however, was despondent and remarked that the embassy attaché assignment was a "dead-end" for his military career. It was not the desired career broadening operational job he was seeking. He wanted so much to make general. Korean retired generals are afforded VIP treatment and benefits and they acquire all of Korea's and US contractors' lucrative defense industry consultant positions, while their retired colonels receive meager retirement incomes and get less prestigious blue-collar jobs.

So Col Chung devised his own "retirement plan." At the time of Col Chung's transfer, the ROK Air Force bought 18 F4E aircraft from the U.S. through the Foreign Military Sales program. When a country purchases military equipment through FMS, the package includes full access to the US supply and follow-on support lines, and the weapons systems have an attractive (cheaper) price tag. These 18 new aircraft were sold to the Koreans for around $10 million each, and the Korean government was contracted to pay for one aircraft per month for 18 months. FMS payments were routinely made through the ROK Embassy's Defense Attaché's office in Washington,

Before the first payment was due, my informant told me that Col Chung wrote an "official" ROK Government letter (signed by the

Defense Attaché Col. Chung) to the US Government requesting a month's delay in payment. The delay, the letter stated, was due to a shortage of foreign exchange dollars in Korea. The friendly US FMS office routinely approved the delay.

Back in Korea, the Korean Government had no knowledge of Col. Chung's "official" letter and the casual U.S. Government's approval for the delay. So when Col Chung received the first $10 mil from his Ministry of National Defense, he immediately deposited the check in a private bank in his name. I'm not sure how he did this. I think he may have bribed the person(s) drawing the checks in Korea to make the check out in his name. For 17 months, Col Chung secretly "earned" the interest off of $10 million plus the dividends from the dividends. Then on the 18th month, he withdrew the $10 mil and made the last payment. Without "stealing" a dollar, he cleverly made a fortune for his retirement.

Col Chung bought a Mercedes-Benz for his D.C. transportation. On one of my official visits to D.C. he treated me to a rather elaborate and expensive Korean dinner.

At the end of his two-year U.S. tour, he and his family did not return to Korea and had apparently disappeared. They may have defected to Canada, and probably are still there. Later someone blew the whistle on Col Chung. A Korean contacted me by phone in Florida and politely asked if I happened to know the whereabouts of the Colonel. He said he was a friend, but I suspected he was Korean CIA. As I truly had no idea, I plead ignorance.

So far, I have heard nothing about what happened to him and his family. Appears from day one, Col. Chung had no intention of returning to Korea.

4. 1978-83 – Following AF retirement, Special Assistant to CEO, Yong Jin Enterprise Co. Manama, Bahrain and Inchon, Korea.

After two years at JUSMAG-Korea, I was reassigned (again) to the Tactical

Air Warfare Center, Eglin AFB FL. This time I was in charge of 250 technicians and engineers as Deputy Chief of Staff for Electronic Warfare Testing. It was purely a staff job, my role was to report to the commanding general the daily test accomplishments. Boring. Then John Lee called and turned my life around. I retired from the Air Force and initiated another career.

I write about my five years working with Koreans and Arabs in Chapter 12.

5.1986-91 – Managing Director, McDonnell-Douglas Korea

After five years together working in the Persian Gulf area, John Lee sold his shares of the company and we both returned home in '83. I was planning to retire when the Analytic Sciences Corp (TASC) called and asked if I would like to be a consultant in their guided weapons program called "Chicken Little." So I worked full-time in missile seeker and warhead testing. Meanwhile, I obtained a Masters degree in Public Administration at University of West Florida, specializing in Defense Systems Acquisition and Contracting.

A few days after graduation, I received a call from McDonnell-Douglas asking if I would like to interview for a managing director job in Korea. I was selected and in June '86 I was back in Seoul, this time as a civilian in a different life style. My job was to market the McAir

F/A-18 aircraft in the Korean fighter program competition. Our major opponent was General Dynamics and its F-16.

I shared an office with Dave Grieshop, the Far East head for MD Helicopters. We had a staff of five outstanding English speaking Korean ladies, two wonderful retired ROKAF generals as consultants, an accountant staff and we were provided cars and personal drivers. My wife and youngest son who accompanied us lived in a four-bedroom three-story condo that MD paid $6500 USD per month rent. Our 3000 sq ft office cost MD $12,000 per month rent.

The Korean Fighter Program (KFP) contract was worth $7.2 billion, involving a 120 aircraft co-production program with Sam Sung Aerospace. It was therefore, a fierce, bloody four-year fight, full of intrigue. Expert marketers from the home offices shuttled back and forth from the home offices with briefings and new data.

The ROK Air Force and the Ministry of National Defense initially selected the F/A-18. It was officially announced that we had won. We celebrated. It was in the newspapers.

I was sent home after the five-year competition and a McDonnell Aircraft Company Vice President replaced me to administer what McD thought was their program.

The victory was short lived as the Korean President at the advice of his Security advisor, reversed the ROKAF/MND selection in favor of the F-16. I speculate that General Dynamics had no knowledge of their Korean agents' promising the Security Advisor a generous part of their commission under the table if the president selected the F-16. Both President, Roh Tae Woo and his Security Advisor were later found guilty of receiving bribery from the large Korean corporations. It was strongly suspected that the KFP reversal was also influenced by money. The ROK government sentenced them with life sentence house arrests.

The investigation and trial took so long (over three years) that the F-16 General Dynamics/Sam Sung co-production KFP program was already well on its way when it was concluded that there was hanky-panky among the Koreans.

The loss of this $7.2 bil sale, along with other marketing failures, contributed to MD Corp caving in to Boeing.

It was exciting times. For instance, while the heated KFP competition was going on, I had the privilege of hosting Senator Dan Inouye of Hawaii and Senator Ted Stevens of Alaska for dinner when they visited Seoul in 1990.

The US Ambassador called me at my office in Seoul to ask me if I could take care of the two visiting US Senators because he had to attend a Korean Foreign Ministry dinner. I was especially pleased because Senator Inouye was a high school classmate of both my brother and his wife May. (McKinley High School, Class of '42 in Honolulu)

A private dinner at the best Korean restaurant was arranged for the senators, who were on this junket as chairman and co-chairman of the Senate Armed Forces Appropriation Committee.

Senator Inouye could only recall my sister-in-law, May, "because she was pretty." Soon after high school graduation, Senator Dan joined the famous 442nd Infantry, made up entirely of Japanese Americans. Because of his proficiency in the Japanese language, my brother served as an interpreter and interrogator.

Over sixty years after the fact, President Clinton belatedly awarded Senator Inouye and several other 442nd Infantry Division heroes the Congressional Medal of Honor for extreme heroism in battle.

Senator Stevens and I talked about our good friend, Lt. General Tom McInerney, who was at that time Commander of the Alaskan Air

Command. I was Lt. McInerney's flight commander some twenty years before at Eglin AFB.

Senators enjoyed the evening as they were hand-fed by the Korean waitresses.

It was an interesting 22 years. My brother and sisters call me the "Korean Kan."

Next: Chapter 12 – The Middle East

CHAPTER 12

THE MIDDLE EAST

On what turned out to be my final tour in the Air Force, I was a Colonel sitting at my desk at Eglin AFB, FL in March of '78, disgruntled that I was no longer flying. I had a prestigious job as a junior Colonel, holding a "Deputy Chief of Staff for Electronic Warfare Testing" position, overseeing 50 or so multi-million dollar test programs and in charge of 200 high tech personnel in my directorate; but it was no fun.

<u>Another turning point in my life:</u>

My secretary buzzed me, interrupting my solitude, and said I had a long-distance call from a guy with a foreign accent. It was my best Korean friend, John Lee, calling from Bahrain. Jung Won "John" Lee had just landed a huge labor contract in that island country in the Persian Gulf. It involved 800 to 1000 Korean laborers performing ground-handling services at the airport, and cargo handling at the seaport.

John asked, "When (do) you retire, Bob?"

"I need you. I (will) double your Colonel salary and (provide) all expenses," he said.

After calling my wife, I went to the commanding generals' office and asked if he would sign a waiver for me to retire immediately, which he did. I retired on 1 April '78 and immediately flew to far away Bahrain to join John Lee.

I called my four-star general advisor, who was then the Air Force Commander in Chief to tell him that I decided to retire. I was a captain and his instructor pilot 14 years before. Earlier on he instructed me to keep in touch and to call him anytime I needed help in getting reassigned to a job or location of choice.

When I told him I was retiring, he hinted, "Don't get out now, Bob, we're promoting more minorities this year." I thanked him and politely declined. I thought to myself, if I stayed in I would prefer to be promoted to general on my personal qualities and achievements and not for my color or race.

The Bahrainis were educated mostly by the Brits, and there were many Scots, Irish, English, Aussies and New Zealanders working for the Bahrain government. Their heavy accents drove the Koreans batty. The Koreans' English was mainly derived from their association with the US Army. They learned the GI's English. The varied English accents they heard in Bahrain sounded quite foreign to them. John Lee was no exception.

As an example, in a heated negotiation session regarding the stevedoring contract at the Bahrain seaport, the Arab Port Director's spokesman, an old English sea captain named John Kendrick said, "You Cahn't, Mr. Lee," in a heavy Brit accent, when John Lee made a proposal at the table.

John turned to me puzzled, and whispered, "Hey Bob, what is 'cahn't'?"

I replied nasally, "He means 'can't,'" I replied.

John Lee could not understand Port Director Eid Abdulla Yousef, because Mr. Yousef was educated at Cambridge University, and he had a distinct British accent. I was there to interpret UK-English to Korean-English and vice-versa, and to explain European cultural idiosyncrasies to John.

When a Brit said, "Let us roll our sleeves up and work together."

John asked, "What mean roll sleeves?" I explained to John that it is a Western saying. The comparable symbology in Korea would be to roll your pant cuffs up (as if preparing to step into and harvest the rice fields). He then understood.

Many idioms had to be explained…"That's water under the bridge," "That's a pie in the sky, Mr. Lee"….all had to be interpreted, as the Koreans took things very literally.

I acted as a trouble-shooter, mostly mending and clarifying communication conflicts between the Koreans and the Arabs. The Koreans learned quickly, and because of their great work ethic they gained the respect of the Arabs in a matter of months, and it resulted in a lucrative five-year project for John Lee.

I was known to the Arab side as the "Korean who speaks like an American."

I once overheard a discussion at an embassy cocktail party between the British Ambassador's wife and the Korean Ambassador's wife about a recent "cinema" they both had seen. I heard the Korean Ambassador's wife say, "Well this guy in the movie bull-shitted his wife, and….." I quickly popped into the conversation, called the Korean lady aside and told her that "bull-shit" isn't nice language, and to use the words "lied" or "deceived," etc. The Korean Ambassador to Bahrain and his wife obviously learned English from their US Army friends in Korea.

In addition to the English, Scots and Irish counterparts, Koreans were introduced to the Palestinians, whom the oil-rich Arabs throughout the Persian Gulf hired as their business managers. The Palestinians were the ones John dealt with on a daily basis, and not the Royal Family Sheikhs (pronounced "shakes"). John became very good friends with a Palestinian named Fouad Habiby, a shrewd but honest man, who was the General Operations Manager at Bahrain Airport. In our Korean company office we hired a Palestinian-American lady named Jasmine "Maggie" Asad, who acted as our liaison and interpreter. Maggie was married to a US Navy Lt. Commander who was a pilot stationed in Bahrain. Maggie expedited much of our basic administrative dealings with the Bahrain government because she was charming and beautiful. Most Americans don't realize that the Arabs treat women very respectively in public. The women are always allowed to be served ahead of men. When Maggie took our visa, work permit or drivers' license applications to the Bahrain city hall, she was welcomed by the supervisor, seated in his office and was served coffee while the paper work was being accomplished by a clerk. Because the clerk was ordered to assist Maggie, the men in line had to wait in line even longer. At closing time, the clerk would say to the men in line: "bukra, mata-asif, in sha-Allah," ("Sorry, perhaps tomorrow, Allah willing.") Maggie always came back with the job done.

Maggie

I never told the Arabs/Palestinians that I had trained with the Israeli Air Force (IAF) in F4 Phantom fighter aircraft, and that I was a good friend of the IAF Chief of Staff, General Avihu Ben Nun. In my association with the IAF and during my five years in the Arab world, I learned of and felt the deep mutual hate they have for each other, and I was at that time convinced that there would never be a peaceful settlement between Israel and Palestine. It is difficult for me to even take sides because both sides have suffered severely at the hands of the other, and who really started it has become irrelevant, no longer pertinent. Contrary to what a lot of my friends think in the USA, there are a lot of ordinary nice people on both sides.

A SIDE STORY – THE BAHRAIN JAIL

I was arrested in Bahrain for DUI. Bahrain, the United Arab Emirates, Oman and Qatar are some of the more liberal Arab countries that allowed bars and alcohol to be served in hotels to expatriots.

I had dinner and a couple of drinks at the Hilton with the DOD school principal and her assistant. Typically, there was a Bahraini motorcycle cop watching people leave the hotel restaurant, and he tailed me. He stopped me and asked me to follow him to the police station. Bahrainis (unlike certain other Arabs) are very gentle, and they got a cab to take the two ladies home compliments of the Bahrain govt. Then they said they would have to retain me overnight because the person who does breathalizer analyses won't be in until morning. So my breath stayed in a balloon overnight. The jailhouse at the police station was new, and quite clean, unlike the ones I saw later in Saudi Arabia when I bailed out some Koreans. (another story)

Clean bunks, sheets and pillow cases, clean floors and they left the cell doors open so all of the retainees could wander about.

One of the guards even gave me a Bahraini coin so I could make a phone call. I called the Korean camp, talked to the General Manager, Mr. Kim. (John Lee was at another function where I was supposed to meet him after I dropped the ladies off). I asked Mr. Kim to send some food and to call Sheikh Hamad bin Rashid Alkhalifa, the chief of police, first thing in the morning. I told Mr. Kim that there were a dozen guys in the jail including a couple of Brits in tennis attire, still holding their tennis rackets in their hands, also in for DUI, a couple of Bahrainis in their typical white attire, two Indians and two Americans from Brown & Root. In about an hour, the guard brought in what the Korean kitchen delivered: a case of oranges, coffee and tuna and egg sandwiches, enough to feed not only the "prisoners," but all of the prison staff.

So I gathered everyone in the center open area, we sat on the floor, ate and talked story. Even a guard sat with us. All were arrested for DUI.

The Brits said they were just leaving the British Club after tennis, and they had a couple of Stouts (beers) each. The Americans were arrogant and indignant and they swore that the police would be in trouble for arresting them...threatening that "they knew the Minister of Commerce." I heard later that they were fined the equivalent of $1500 each. One Indian was so funny. I asked him why he was in the jail, and he said in perfect English, "Well sir, I live in Awali (where many Indian laborers lived in shacks around junkyards full of abandoned cars) and after work I was drinking one bottle of beer sitting in an old Mercedes Benz with no wheels. A policeman happened to drive by and saw me, and arrested me citing me for 'drinking while in command of a vehicle.' " He apparently was arrested by a cop with a sense of humor, and was eventually released in the AM with no fine. He thanked me and said that it was a lucky day for him, having free food from the Koreans and a nice bed for the night. Actually, Bahrain's rather liberal law allows alcohol, but not to be consumed in public.

Well at about 2:00AM everyone went to bed.

Around 8:00AM I heard the guard, "Robert Kan, please come to the office."

Apparently John Lee got hold of Sheikh Hamad, and Hamad got the word to the station. They politely handed me my '83 Honda Accord keys and cordially dismissed me.

The Alkhalifas are the ruling royalty of Bahrain. Sheikh Hamad and his brother, Sheikh Isa bin Rashid (son of Rashid) Alkhalifa were John Lee's good friends. They are first cousins of the Amir (King).

It was a fun evening. The school principal and her assistant were quite relieved when I told them about my night in jail.

Roosters from India Crowed at 2 A.M. in Bahrain.

In Bahrain, I made an important discovery in animal husbandry regarding the brain of the rooster. The thousands of laborers from India were allowed to bring their live chickens to Bahrain. They were allowed to raise chickens on the roofs of their apartment houses for eggs and meat. These crowded government furnished living quarters were in a complex within earshot from where I lived in my two-bedroom flat.

I was awakened every morning at 2 A.M. by what seemed like fifty roosters crowing. They would start about 1:45 A.M. and crow for about a half-hour, every morning in the dark. I eventually figured out that the roosters' body clock was not adjustable. Bombay is 3 hours ahead of Bahrain. It is 5 A.M. in Bombay, so it is the proper time for Indian roosters to crow regardless where they are.

I want to one day bring a rooster home to Florida from California to see if it would crow at 8 A.M.

An unforgettable friend:

When I got to Bahrain in '78, one of the sources of information regarding local business and politics was to talk to the commercial attaché at the US Embassy. The attaché turned out to be 32-year-old Dr. Laraine Carter, who eventually became one of my best friends in my life.

She was most enthusiastic, an extremely vivacious, fun person. She was brilliant. Laraine had a law degree with a Ph.D. in Islamic Law, a social sciences masters degree, and a bachelors in Spanish. She taught me so much about the Arab people, economics and politics, and she loved to talk about flying because she herself was a licensed pilot and enjoyed my "war stories." She loved Korean food.

Note: I write in the past tense, and saying "was" because Laraine passed away in 2006.

Her father was a diplomat and she grew up in Abu Dhabi, UAE, and was schooled with the Royal Family children. She was a good friend of Sheik Sayed bin Sultan, the Amir of Abu Dhabi and the former president of the UAE. As a result of this exposure, Laraine became completely fluent in written and spoken Arabic. She later became fluent in Spanish, and could converse in Farsi (Iranian), Afghan and Italian. She obviously became a valuable asset to the US government during the Iraq conflicts.

The Spanish Ambassador in Bahrain thought Laraine was from Spain because Laraine spoke Spanish like a native.

When she left Bahrain, she was assigned to the US mission in Bogota, Columbia.

In her impeccable Spanish she was very much at home there.

Back in the USA, Laraine assumed the role of teaching US government officials badly needed lessons in Arab culture. There weren't too many Americans with her in-depth qualifications. She had a rank of SES (senior executive service -- rank equivalent of Major General).

Just before she died, she was shuttling back and forth from D.C. to Iraq with State & Defense Department officials. She died mysteriously of "food-poisoning" after returning from Iraq. Her offices would not provide details.

The USA lost one of its National Treasures.

Dr. Laraine

Next: Chapter 13 – Celebrities

CHAPTER 13

MEETING CELEBRITIES:

JOHN WAYNE:

For five years I had a summer job as a stacker of cans at the Dole Pineapple cannery where my Mom worked. I had a second job in the evening at the Queen's Hospital in Honolulu as a "gopher" at the Emergency Ward. I assisted the doctors and nurses, fetching medicines, towels, wheel chairs; and was trained to help move patients from cars and ambulances on to stretchers. I became friends with several resident doctors, and even earned money teaching them basic ukulele chords. I befriended a resident physician named Dr. Earle Meuli, who later changed his named to "Maile." He would play a major part in the direction of my life's path eight years later as an Air Force Flight Surgeon.

It was in this setting that I got to meet John Wayne. He was filming the movie "Big Jim McClain," (his worst movie ever, released in '52) and he came to the hospital to visit his director who was suddenly hospitalized. One of my jobs was to keep people out of the doctors' parking lot. One evening I heard a familiar voice, "Where can I park, son?" It was John Wayne.

I recognized "the Duke" immediately, and asked him to leave the car with me, and I parked it out of the way in the medical staff parking lot. He visited daily for about ten evenings, and I took care of him each night. When his director was released from the hospital, he said "this is my last visit, Son, how about coming down to Queen's Surf after work and have a drink with us?" He palmed a $20 bill (BIG BUCKS in the '50s) when he shook my hand and thanked me. My nurse boss allowed me to take off early and I took a bus to Waikiki making my way to the Queen's Surf lounge and found him with his movie crew. He introduced me to his friends, all movie staffers, but none of his co-stars were there. He treated me to a beer and a club sandwich. Don't remember the conversation, but he was very cordial and polite. (No one dared to ask me my age because I was with John Wayne.)

Some of the nurses at the hospital, including my sister Kats, and classmate Millie Oishi were perturbed with me because I didn't call them so they could talk to, or just even peek at John Wayne and that I failed to get his autograph.

Soon after, I left Hawaii at the old age of 19, to attend New York University.

TENESSEE ERNIE FORD

In '64 one of our squadron pilots, Pete Hayes, was getting married in Palo Alto. So four of us scheduled a "navigation, air-refueling and instrument training mission" in two F4C aircraft from Eglin AFB FL to Moffett NAS CA, where Pete was getting married on that weekend in April. Pete grew up as Ernie's neighbor in Menlo Park, near Stanford U. Ern was happy to sing at Pete & Carol's wedding.

Ern sang "Because," and "I Love You Truly," so beautifully there was not a dry eye in the crowd. After the noon-time wedding, Ern invited us Air Force guys to his house for a cocktail party as the wedding couple took off to Monterey for their honeymoon. Ern hosted the impromptu party pool-side and we had a great time. I took this photo at the wedding:

Ern extended an invitation for me to use his penthouse apartment at the Waikiki Colony Surf Hotel when I returned from my Southeast Asia assignment, and invited me to call him anytime I was in the neighborhood.

After I retired from the Air Force, while en route on Round-the-World business trips I stopped overnight in SFO on two occasions to see Ern and wife Betty, who would always welcome me to drive down to their home in Palo Alto from SFO airport. He enjoyed talking to fighter pilots.

He and Mary once came over to my house in Kailua to have huli-huli chicken with my family out in the backyard, and he sang Hawaiian songs for us as I accompanied him on the ukulele. He of course came over in Aloha shirt and slippers. My Mom was amazed what big feet Ern had.

When I got back from my combat tour in '66, Ern and Betty were in Honolulu and wife Nan and I were invited for dinner with them at Michelles at the Colony Surf. Ern introduced me to escargot that evening.

Much later, when Lt. Pete Hayes became Brigadier General Hayes, Pete flew Ernie in an F-15 at Nellis AFB NV. I received a teasing call from Ernie..."Guess what, Bob? Eat your heart out.... I went straight up today!" He was thrilled.

Ernie died a few years ago. Ern's son, Buck, is perpetuating the legend of "Sixteen Tons" and "Bless your pea-pickin' heart."

JAMES S. MCDONNELL – FOUNDER MCDONNELL AIRCRAFT CO. & CORPORATION

I was assigned to Headquarters Pacific Air Forces (PACAF) as the F4 Requirements Officer when I returned from my combat tour in Southeast Asia. I was responsible for defining and formalizing the current mission needs of our combat forces in the form of Southeast Asia operational requirements. In the process I attended many F4 Requirements and Modification Conferences. One such conference was held in the spring of '67 at the McDonnell-Douglas Corporation plant in St. Louis chaired by Col. JJ Burns (Lt.Gen ret). During the conference, I was beckoned by MDC Chairman and founder, James

S. McDonnell to his office for a chat. He was the greatest advocate of the safety of having two engines on a fighter aircraft, and he had heard that I was able to survive a missile hit in North Vietnam because of a second engine and he wanted to hear my story. He was affectionately known as "Mr. Mac," and he intently listened to my story. He was so warm and cordial. He was delighted to hear that after our right engine was killed by the missile fragments, the left engine ran long enough for us to get out of harm's way to bail out on safe grounds. He then took me on a personal tour of the F4 assembly line. I heard later that it was rare for anyone to be taken on a tour by the Chairman Mr. "Mac." He is a legend among the aviation pioneers, like Glenn Martin, Howard Hughes and Donald W. Douglas.

Little did I realize that I would be working for McDonnell-Douglas Corporation 19 years later.

James S. McDonnell -Chairman

APPOLO 12 ASTRONAUT
CHARLES "PETE" CONRAD

I have mentioned my work as Managing Director at the McDonnell Douglas-Korea representing McAir, co-working with McHelicopters Managing Director Dave Grieshop ('86-'91). Occasionally, senior corporate management would come to Korea to check our marketing progress. One of the more delightful and inspiring visitors was the Corporate Vice President for Marketing, Charles "Pete" Conrad, the Appolo pilot who made the second landing on the moon in November '69. It was described as a "pin-point landing." I believe he told me that the computer that guided his landing "with small manual corrections," had a memory of 64K.

I had the pleasure of accompanying Pete to other MD offices in Hong Kong, Singapore and Tokyo. He had a million interesting stories. Pete was a USN F4B fighter pilot with much combat time in North Vietnam, so we had something in common. As with most of the astronauts he had a great sense of humor.

Pete - Appolo 12

Corporate VP Pete Conrad in my MDKorea office.

How I met Bob Hope. See Chapter 9 – Vietnam

Next: Chapter 14 – Holes In One Stories

CHAPTER 14

HOLE-IN-ONE STORIES

Someone once said:

"Man blames fate for other accidents, but feels personally responsible when he makes a hole in one."

That "magic" happened to me three times...have had 3 aces, 12 years apart. '64, '76 and '88. I was expecting to get a hole-in-one in the year 2000, and was disappointed that it didn't happen. Perhaps in year 2012 ......??.

1964: ACTUALLY, I cheated.....NOT AN OFFICIAL ACE. IT WAS A PAR BECAUSE I HIT THE FIRST SHOT INTO THE WATER. HOWEVER, THE FIRST WET SHOT WAS DEEMED A "Mulligan" AFTER THE SECOND WAS HOLED. This shot was at the 156 yard Par 3 Eglin GC, mostly over water.

I hit a 7 iron perfectly. (dem were DA days!) It hit on the green, rolled a few yards before it dropped. There were seven witnesses. Traditionally the one who gets a hole-in-one buys drinks for anyone around. I think it cost me only about $25 when we finished.

<u>1976:</u> On #16 205 yard Par 3 at Yong San 8th Army GC in Seoul. Playing with 15 year old son David, Army Capt John Goble, and an Army civil service guy. I hit a 4-wood high against the wind and the ball amazingly slam-dunked directly in the hole on the fly without touching the green. Good friend Air Force Brigadier Gen Garry Willard was playing ahead with two Korean generals on the next tee. They all heard my ball hitting the pin.

It was in the late afternoon on Dec 31st and it was traditional to close the golf course bar and restaurant early to allow the Korean employees to go home to prepare for the New Year; so I was spared buying all customary drinks and food after play.

As the word spread, I was pressed to buy drinks at the Senior Officers' Club later that evening at its New Year's celebration.

<u>1988</u>: As McDonnell Douglas Regional Manager and friend of the ROK AF, I was invited to play in a USAF vs. ROKAF golf tournament at Osan AB with good friends, 4 star general Chief-of-Staff Suh Dong Yul and BGen Peter Hayes who was the acting commander of the USAF 2nd Air Division playing in the tournament.

On hole #2, a shortened par 4 due to construction, I hit a three wood 225 yards; it hit the front of the green and rolled another 25 yards into the hole.

As a result, I was obligated to buy drinks AND FOOD, for all 72 participants at the awards banquet following the tournament. Korean custom.

Old friend John Lee was also playing in the tournament. He was the concessionaire owner of the Osan golf course restaurant and bar. When John heard that I had a hole-in-one he told General Suh that he would provide all the food gratis, and Bob Kan would only buy the drinks. John defrayed the cost of my ace by paying about 75% of the total cost, and just charged me $400 (a discount). Both Air Force officials were very delighted that we provided free booze and food for the military participants.

Small world...John Lee, the golf course restaurant owner, was my best friend in Korea...Met John when I was flying from Yokota, Japan TDY to Osan in '70-'71, then as Squadron Commander at Kunsan in '72-'73 where John owned the Korean restaurant on base there; later worked for him in Bahrain....and in '88 we're sharing the party expenses at Osan AB for 72 Americans and Koreans blue-suiters.

Then there was 314th Air Division Vice-Commander, BGen Hayes.... Lt Pete Hayes was a F4 backseater at Eglin in '64-'65, I attended his wedding when TN Ernie Ford sang and partied with us....23 years later Pete & I are playing golf with the ROKAF Chief of Staff.....(see photo in Chapter 13 – Celebrities)

So at a table for ten, John Lee, Pete Hayes and I had dinner with Gen Suh and other retired 4 star Korean Generals I knew from the past. In addition, the Mayor of the nearby town was present. Lots of "dup-si-DA" (bottoms up). Stayed at Pete's quarters that night.

Most golfers wish for just one hole-in-one in their lifetimes. It's hard to believe I made three.

(I keep conveniently forgetting the first one was really a par.)

It is great to buy a keg of beer to celebrate an ace in the USA. However, it's painful and expensive in Korea and Japan, and most golfers there have Hole-In-one insurance as one is obligated to buy everyone dinner and drinks.

Social coercion is the only force behind it. I never heard of anyone not buying after a hole-in-one.

LOOKING FORWARD TO MANY MORE "HOLES-IN-ONE" FIGURATIVELY AND LITERALLY IN MY FUTURE…..

Next: Chapter 15 – Explanation: "Not Really an American"

CHAPTER 15

"NOT REALLY AN AMERICAN"

Many of us from Hawaii have these experiences when traveling abroad.

Mainly, we will hear, "You speak good English."

Here are a few encounters on what I now consider humorous anecdotes that illustrate some of the racial-national misunderstandings and misconceptions. It involves people who think Americans are only either White or Black and all other minorities are 1st generation immigrants.

Note: I emphasize that as an Asian-American with 22 years of military service, I never encountered any racial prejudice in the US Air Force. I have not seen the kind of indignities my Black, Jewish or Hispanic friends have experienced in their own lives and communities.

I always have appreciated the fact that my friends and associates treated me as an individual, Bob Kan, Officer, Fighter Pilot, Gentleman (perhaps), and nothing else.

Of course, sensitivities depend on the individual. I'd like to think that I have not been defensive or over-sensitive.

<u>Story #1:</u> The term, "Not really an American," came from a relatively recent conversation I had on the golf course with a retired Air Force Lt. Colonel.

It was a typical Saturday. He was my golf partner that day, and during the course of play, he asked if I knew one of his old squadron buddies, "A JAPANESE named Wilfred Watanabe."

Yes, I knew Wilfred. We played high school ball together in Honolulu. I immediately attempted to correct him, explaining that "Wilfred is not just Japanese. He is an American, of Japanese ancestry."

To which the old guy abruptly replied, "WELL, HE'S NOT A REAL AMERICAN."

I persisted explaining that Wilfred left the Air Force to attend law school and after many years of successful practice he was appointed the Supreme Court Justice for the State of Hawaii.

(I heard him mutter under his breath, "Well, he's still NOT REALLY AN AMERICAN.")

<u>Story #2:</u> Just recently I was having a drink at the Eglin AFB golf course nineteenth hole lounge with one of our good friends from South Korea, a widow of a retired American civil servant. She is a naturalized American citizen, very attractive, well-educated and speaks English without a foreign accent. We were making small talk, and I told her I was going to a Honolulu high school class of '50 reunion in a couple of weeks, and showed her photos of some of my classmates.

One photo was of the lovely Jeannie Anderson, a classmate since the first grade and still the beautiful and charming blonde at 75.

Jeannie Anderson

The lady was astonished, pointing to Jeannie's photo, "This lady is your classmate?" I acknowledged, "Yes."

"But she's an American."….she said.

<u>Story #3:</u> At an Air Force Special Forces cocktail party at the Hurlburt AFB Officers' Club in 1996, there were some high-ranking Laotian officers in attendance as guests of honor. During the cocktail hour before dinner, I was conversing with a young Air Force Captain and his pretty blonde wife. I had on a VIETNAM VETERAN lapel pin, which the Captain's wife noticed. She inquired: "You were in the Vietnam War?" I said "Yes, I was."

She just about knocked me for a loop when she then asked: "Which side were you on?" (I'm not kidding)

It later occurred to me that she wasn't yet born when I was flying in Vietnam.

<u>Story #4:</u> Mistaken for a Japanese Gardner – I'm sure many Asian-Americans have faced similar situations.….

It was in the summer of 1970. We were settled down in the US Air Force housing compound called Kanto Mura about ten miles west of downtown Tokyo. I was assigned as Chief of the Fighter Training Branch at Headquarters 5th Air Force, Fuchu Air Base, Japan. I was a Major soon to be promoted to Lt. Col.

Our family, wife Nan, two daughters and a son, moved into a two story three bedroom apartment where some 120 Air Force military and civilian families resided. These Americans supported Headquarters 5th Air Force, US Air Force at Tachikawa Air Base, and three Army garrisons.

Each occupant of government housing had the responsibility of maintaining a portion of the lawn surrounding the apartment complex. Housing supply provided unpowered, old-fashioned lawn mowers.

It was a hot summer day, and I rolled a thin wet towel and tied it in a band around my head, Japanese style. I wore some old shorts and a t-shirt.

As I was mowing back and forth in front of our apartment, a petite young wife from the next apartment building came over to me and asked me (quite animated), gesturing and pointing at the lawn mower and the lawn, "Mister, how much you charge to cut grass?" She spoke slowly and enunciated each word...

Having had such experiences in similar scenarios before, I knew she thought I was a Japanese yardman.

So I pointed to my wife who happened to be sitting on the front steps watching me work, and I said in broken English, "You see lady? She no pay me money...She pay me in bed...I sleep with her. Okay with you?"

The young lady, a former airline hostess and the wife of a fighter pilot friend, looked at me incredulously, and then scurried away in a hurry. Her husband and I laughed about it later, but I suspect to this day she has not forgiven me for playing that joke on her. (Sorry, Ellie!)

Story #5: Home of Record

I got my combat assignment to Vietnam in early November '65 to join the 433ʳᵈ Fighter Squadron at George AFB in mid-December. When assigned to a remote (unaccompanied) tour, the military member's family and household goods are routinely transported to their "home of record." When I got my orders, I got an appointment with a base transportation officer to arrange for the move. When the Capt. transportation officer heard me declare that Honolulu was my home of record, he said it couldn't be done because Hawaii was "overseas," and this was not allowed. So I spoke to his boss, then his boss's boss, and finally the issue had to go to the Tactical Air Command Headquarters for approval. The request approval process dragged on for weeks, and my reporting date was approaching. About a week before I was to deploy, I still had no port call for my family, although the household goods were already picked up.

I didn't want my family "on the road" when I started flying combat missions so I took it upon myself to send my wife and three kids home commercially at my own expense. Later I found out their port call at Travis AFB to fly to Hawaii was on December 19ᵗʰ, the very day I got shot down in North Vietnam.

After I miraculously survived and was rescued (see Chapter 9) I applied for reimbursement from the USAF. Even after several appeals, my request for reimbursement was refused because it was "unauthorized transportation." I was flying combat missions so I couldn't concentrate on writing letter after letter to some ignorant Colonel at the Pentagon who regarded Hawaii as some foreign country. The US Government still owes me $1500. Can you imagine that happening to any of our Military today?

However, I am not one to hold a grudge. I am not forgetting the many wonderful and positive "breaks" and favorable considerations I have been afforded by the Air Force, which in my mind tends to offset administrative blunders.

Story #6: Air Rescue in Vietnam

The most dramatic experience of misidentification of nationality happened to me in December of '65 during rescue operations after Joe Moran and I bailed out after a Soviet SA-2 Surface-to-Air-Missile (SAM) near Hanoi hit us. There is a detailed description of this episode in Chapter 9 of this document.

The Jolly Green rescue team initially rejected rescuing me and departed because I looked like the enemy, and only returned to pick me up after I voiced my displeasure in no uncertain terms over the hand-held emergency radio.

It's now a laughable incident, but it would not have been funny had the helicopter left me in Northern Laos.

Not the end.

BOB KAN, BORN OCTOBER 26, 1932.

Bob is a 3rd Generation Japanese-American (JA) born and raised in Hawaii. As a 7-year-old, Bob told his Mom he wanted to be a pilot. As a nine-year old, he witnessed Japan's attack on Pearl Harbor. Bob was selling newspapers on the streets of Honolulu to soldiers and sailors, many in Hawaii on their way to fight the enemy forces in the Pacific, while Japanese American volunteers were fighting and dying in European battles as part of the 442nd and 100th infantry units to prove that they were, indeed, REAL AMERICANS, loyal to the United States even though their ethnicity was that of an enemy nation. Many served while their families were incarcerated by the US government behind barbed wire in the deserts of Utah and Arizona. Those heroic soldiers did pave the way for succeeding generation JAs like Bob to obtain his pilot wings and eventually earn the rank of Colonel, USAF, without prejudice. He became a jet pilot instructor and subsequently flew 168 combat missions in the F4C Phantom. In 1965 Bob was shot down over North Vietnam and rescued by a helicopter. In '72 he was assigned as one of the first Japanese-American Fighter Squadron Commanders in the USAF. During his military career, he befriended and worked with the Israeli, Australian, UK, Japanese and Korean Air Forces. Bob's background led to interesting international ventures after his retirement from active duty Air Force that exceeded his imagination or expectations. For five years he worked in the Middle East with Koreans, Arabs and Europeans and was later a Managing Director of McDonnel-Douglas Korea in Seoul, Korea. He is now on an extended coffee break.

CPSIA information can be obtained
at www.ICGtesting.com
Printed in the USA
FFOW02n0239081114
8626FF